WHO OWNS POVERTY?

PRAISE FOR THIS BOOK

"A meditation on poverty that goes profoundly deeper than anyone else has gone. It's a revelation to find that materialism does not get at the nature of human misery any more than it gets at human happiness. This book will bring major changes in public policy."

—Edmund Phelps, 2006 Nobel Laureate in Economics;
Director, Center on Capitalism and Society, Columbia University

"Not just a new contribution to development literature but a new paradigm for effective change. Burt is eminently qualified to offer a better way of influencing dramatic and sustainable economic, psychological and social progress for the world's most vulnerable. Those entrenched in old funding and program models will find this book irritating. Those whose first commitment is to results rather than legacy models will find it illuminating. Open. Read. And learn from one of the world's most effective influencers."

—Joseph Grenny, New York Times bestselling co-author
of Influencer and Crucial Conversations

"A wonderful account of the work of Fundación Paraguaya, which runs perhaps the most effective anti-poverty program anywhere in the world. It is an absorbing, compelling story of the lessons learned in its widely-successful fight against poverty—and, most importantly, the profound lessons the world can learn from the Foundation in this most fundamental, necessary, and compassionate of all human endeavors."

—Ken Wilber, Author of The Theory of Everything and
The Religion of Tomorrow

"This book is poised to make a significant contribution to the critical task of rethinking conventional assumptions about what poverty is, and how it can be eliminated. Burt weaves a compelling case that what poverty is varies from household to household; the knowledge and creativity of those experiencing poverty are critical to solving it; and long-neglected perspectives from the South are as important as those from the North. This book should be on every development syllabus, and on the nightstand of everyone working to end poverty."

–Richard Matthew, Faculty Director, Blum Center for Poverty Alleviation, University of California Irvine

"Having worked in social development for the past 40 years— I am excited with how Burt defines and simplifies poverty, and places it where it belongs… in the family. It's too limited to see the Stoplight as an assessment tool; it's an intervention tool as well, providing the family a development plan, and giving them the agency to take charge. I have seen it firsthand through our work with the Poverty Stoplight within the WDB Zenzele Development Programme."

–Zanele Mbeki, Social worker and Founder, Women's Development Banking Trust (South Africa)

"This book and the Poverty Stoplight are game-changers. They remind you that, wherever you are in the world, you have the opportunity to help end poverty, not reduce it, but end it. Who wouldn't want the key to that door?"

–Lyla Bashan, Author of Global: An Extraordinary Guide for Ordinary Heroes

"A profoundly important book and long overdue. It challenges the orthodoxy of largely unsuccessful top-down prescriptions for measuring and 'ameliorating' poverty (whatever that means), offering an alternative rooted in the lived experience and entrepreneurial spirit of the poor. It is a compelling account, a space for new and profound conversations."

–James Koch, Founding Fellow and Emeritus Professor, Miller Center for Social Entrepreneurship, Santa Clara University

"Martín Burt fundamentally reframes the way we think about poverty. When poor families are welcomed into the process of designing solutions to the world's thorniest challenges, they become the protagonists of their own stories. Drawing on decades of experience as a mayor, an academic, and a development practitioner, Burt offers a road map for working with the world's poor to eliminate poverty for good. A must-read for all people who are fighting for transformational change.

–*Willy Foote, Founder and CEO, Root Capital (US)*

"A powerful reminder that good intentions will not solve global poverty. Poor people themselves must be involved in defining and solving their own poverty, and their voices must be heard in development organizations. His book documents how this can happen with the Poverty Stoplight. The Poverty Stoplight honors the potential of human creativity and resourcefulness."

–*Margee Ensign, President, Dickinson College*

"Martín Burt is a remarkable changemaker, equally at home in rural villages of Paraguay or Tanzania as in Davos. This book is a wonderful account of his personal journey exploring how to make poverty measurement genuinely 'owned' by the poor in ways that expand their agency to potentially transform the nature of their interaction with state and market institutions. This story is vividly told, right down to the dialogues of engagement and resistance that he faced on this ongoing exploration."

–*Michael Walton, Senior Lecturer in Public Policy, Harvard Kennedy School*

"A marvelous book, beautifully written. Overflowing with wisdom, humility, clear and revolutionary bottom-up philosophy and methodology for eliminating poverty in partnership with families and communities. It is filled with fascinating stories about addressing the resistance to change and the addiction to conventional wisdom embedded in government. Every anti-poverty activist, advocate, or administrator needs to read this book."

–*Dorothy Stoneman, Founder, YouthBuild (US)*

"Such powerful reflections and insights about an undeniable reality: that no one knows more about poverty than those who experience it, and that external solutions can only concentrate on the appearance of poverty, rather than its essence. So too is it a powerful challenge to those organizations working on the Sustainable Development Goals—a call to return ownership of (and power over) poverty to those whose lives it shapes, and to ensure that the opportunities they supply match the demands made by poor families themselves."

—Carmen Velasco, Co-Founder, ProMujer International

"This book is a masterpiece. Its power is the lens it creates through which assumptions are challenged and new perspectives are formed. If a problem well-defined is a problem half-solved, this book is a testament to how we view and define the problem can either liberate or limit us. A must-read read by all who have a conscience and are advocates for a more just and fair society."

—Diran Apelian, Alcoa-Howmet Professor of Engineering, Worcester Polytechnic Institute; Distinguished Visiting Professor, University of California Irvine

"Martín has a unique ability to see solutions where others see only problems, solutions that begin with empowering people by enabling them to see that they are capable of what no one else thinks they can do: defining their own biggest challenges and then triumphing over them. And when a few people do that, then an entire village starts to do it, and entire nations and maybe even the world."

—Carl Byker, Winner of the Primetime Emmy and Peabody awards

"Martín Burt devotes his entire life to understanding and alleviating poverty. His methodologies are pragmatic and adaptive. His heart is magnanimous, sharing all his knowledge selflessly. You will certainly gain from reading this rich depository of wisdom."

—Jack Sim, Founder, World Toilet Organization (Singapore)

"Burt's life long quest to understand and abolish poverty is inspirational. This beautifully-written, engrossing book makes the case that the only path to poverty elimination is to put the real experts, people living in poverty, at the center of the solution. This book will leave you with a glowing feeling that poverty could soon be relegated to the past."

—Dr. Jordan Kassalow, Founder, VisionSpring;
Co-Founder, EYElliance (US)

"This book argues convincingly that it is essential to account for the knowledge, talent, views and experience of the people subject to the problem of poverty in order for the effort and resources of governments and development organizations to be successful in overcoming that poverty."

—Vicky Colbert, Founder and Director,
Fundación Escuela Nueva (Colombia)

"This book powerfully calls us to make a bet on who can best stamp out poverty: people who grapple with the challenges of poverty every day. At a moment in the life of our world when we need to come together across divides to create positive change, it shares inspiring stories that illumine a new, transformative way to understand and tackle poverty."

—J.B. Schramm, Co-Founder, PeerForward (US)

"Eliminating poverty is an audacious aspiration. Martín Burt shows how it could be achieved. This inspiring, page-turning narrative is a must-read for development practitioners in NGOs and charities, for local and national politicians; indeed for anyone who is prepared to have their thinking challenged and their development practice disrupted."

—Robert Webb, Director of Transmit Enterprise CIC;
Director of UK Poverty Stoplight Hub, SIGNAL

"A delightfully readable book, with language that is luminous and flashes of humor throughout. The time-worn clichés about poverty are far too narrow, top-down, too simplistic. This book tells the story of Martín's gradually-evolving revolutionary approach to eliminating poverty, a journey that takes him all over the world, to the Corporate Social Responsibility giants of the private sector to the poorest of the poor in the slums."

—Dr. Taddy Blecher, CEO, Maharishi Invincibility Institute (South Africa)

"A generous invitation to understand and learn from an incredible journey dedicated to impact communities as a changemaker. While sharing his deep questions about the concept of poverty, Martín offers us a chance to be more successful in our attempts to work and fight against social injustice. The Poverty Stoplight is an innovative approach to empower families and communities to eliminate their own poverty. Revealing his great storytelling talent, Martín explains how we can unite efforts to make it happen, and how to put people at the center."

—Rodrigo Baggio, President and Founder, Center for Digital Inclusion (Brazil)

"This book will become an indispensable manual, and can potentially change the perspective of millions of people, its effects reaching into the most secluded corners of the planet to change the destiny that for centuries fell as the worst punishment to humanity."

—Luis Szaran, Founder, Sounds of the Earth (Paraguay)

WHO OWNS POVERTY?

MARTIN BURT

Red Press
Who Owns Poverty?
Dr. Martín Burt

Printed in Chicago by Versa Press
Typeset in Garamond

Published by Red Press Ltd.
ISBN 978 1 912157 129 (Paperback)
ISBN 978 1 912157 136 (Ebook)

A catalogue record for this book is available from the British Library

Red Press Registered Offices:
6 Courtenay Close, Wareham, Dorset, BH20 4ED, England
www.redpress.co.uk
@redpresspub

#WhoOwnsPoverty
#PovertyStoplight

To Dorrie, the love of my life.

CONTENTS

INTRODUCTION

W HAT IF NEARLY EVERYTHING we thought we knew about poverty was wrong? What if the legions of policymakers, social scientists, economists, aid workers, charities and NGOs marching across the globe have been using the wrong strategy, and the wrong tactics, to wage the wrong war against poverty? With the very best of intentions, we've been trying to help poor people ascend the ladder out of poverty in the name of social and economic justice. But what if we have been, as it were, leaning the wrong ladder on the wrong wall? And what if being wrong about the problem of poverty was the only thing standing in the way of finding the solution?

Of course, this would not be the first time that society labored under assumptions later proved to be misguided. Recall a time when educators believed that corporal punishment would 'cure' left-handed students, long before we understood that handedness is determined *in utero*. Doctors in ages past believed tuberculosis to be transmitted by vampires – and that dry air in caves, deserts or mountains was a potent cure – before scientists determined it is caused by bacteria and therefore best treated with antibiotics. Before Copernicus and Galileo, scientists believed the sun revolved around the earth.

1

Nor have our views on poverty itself been immune to similar debate and revision. Seeking to justify the persistent gap between rich countries and poor countries, theorists over the ages have proffered explanations ranging from the cultural to the geographical—and most everything in between.

Marxists view poverty as the inevitable result of the uneven distribution of the means of producing wealth in a society. Capitalism was created to organize production in the belief that enlightened self-interest and the logic of the market create wealth for all; it depended on a certain measure of wealth inequality to promote the entrepreneurial spirit and risk-taking behavior needed to create more jobs and more wealth (and on the view that government programs to reduce inequality only got in the way). Indeed, it's only in recent years that we've started to challenge the orthodoxy of inequality as a necessary precondition for growth.

Elsewhere, the Bible assures us that the poor will always be with us, and the Protestant work ethic reminds us the poor only have themselves to blame—as wealth (the outward sign of God's blessing) is achieved by overcoming personal, moral, intellectual or spiritual deficits. And if our hard work means we deserve our wealth, the converse must also be true: we deserve our poverty when it happens.

While these worldviews proffer competing narratives on why there is poverty, they are strangely silent on the question of what poverty actually is—as if, perhaps, we are meant to infer the definition from context. But surely if we're going to get serious about the business of reducing global poverty, then we've got to start by agreeing what we mean by the term, right? Here, too, we witness the evolution of human understanding over time.

In our earliest attempts to define poverty, we alighted on the most straightforward of answers. Poverty must be a lack of money: a lack of money coming in (income) and a lack of money going out (consumption). Poverty is the opposite of profit, wealth and accumulation—all of the things society values as inherently good. Armed with this understanding, our solution was to throw money at the problem—in the form of alms, conditional cash transfers and (more circuitously) trickle-down economics.

When our progress in global poverty reduction hit a plateau, we went back to first principles. Some converted poverty from a problem into an opportunity; witness poor Bangladeshi and Mexican women rebranded as 'microentrepreneurs' and offered microloans to grow their cottage industries and thereby increase their income. For those tinkering with the engine of economic growth, this was a thrilling retrofit designed to harness the potential energy of poor individuals, to unleash the power of small business and to empower women as economic agents—by giving them the skills, incentives and motivation they lacked to make enough money to live well.

Still others looked beyond the question of cash to reimagine poverty as a many-faced beast. We started talking about 'multidimensional poverty', which encompassed a lack of voice, access, equality, security, health, sanitation, education, infrastructure, political representation and so much more. Yet while this new multidimensional framework accounted for a broad range of societal, structural and political factors that created and maintained poverty, income was still at the top of the list. Income was, quite simply, seen as a key that automatically unlocked well-being improvements across the board.

Our current definition of multidimensional poverty, however, comes preloaded with two unsettling consequences. These consequences shape our understanding of what causes poverty and, as a result, what we can do about it.

To understand the first of these, let's consider the Sustainable Development Goals (SDGs), elaborated by the United Nations (UN). The primary goal is 'No Poverty' (largely defined in terms of income and access to resources), and a further 16 goals consider hunger; health; education; gender inequality; water and sanitation; clean and affordable energy; work and economic growth; industry, innovation and infrastructure; sustainable cities; responsible consumption and production; climate change and environmental degradation; and peace and justice.

There's nothing inherently wrong with getting everyone in the development sector working from the same definition and toward the same goals. It's the manner in which the SDGs are formulated that creates the problem. That's because when one person's poverty is partly, or even wholly, subject to forces beyond their control, we negate the efficacy of any individual effort in overcoming that poverty. I might, if I were living in poverty, be able to increase my income, but I have zero influence over structural factors that mitigate my ability to improve my life and livelihood, such as trade distortions in global agricultural markets, my country's resilience to climatic events and respect for the rule of law, or whether the Ministry of Health provides adequate funding for my local hospital.

In short: the way we define poverty makes it too complex to solve. While we've long since abandoned the idea that a person's poverty is their fault (because they are too uneducated, lazy or apathetic to provide for themselves), there's little room within the current paradigm for a poor person to have any agency over most of the factors that create their poverty. It's too big. Too difficult to influence. Out of their hands. Reliance on external solution-providers is baked in, by design.

The second unsettling consequence of the current definition of multidimensional poverty is that it renders development organizations' current, unidimensional solutions obsolete. Development organizations, by nature, typically focus on one or two issues; despite recognizing that there are many interlocking pieces to the puzzle, we only work on one of them, leaving the rest to someone else. We dig wells and build bridges. We hand out shoes. We train journalists. We administer vaccines. We help farmers grow bigger harvests without worrying about whether they can get their crops to market. We empower the women without bringing the men along for the journey toward a more gender-equal society. We work on decreasing child mortality but leave building schools to someone else. We might win the battle, but we'll never win the war.

At the same time, no one can doubt that poverty – however we define, measure and tackle it – is a growing threat to existing institutions and the cause of much unnecessary suffering in the world. Poverty, abject and otherwise, also manifests as increasing levels of broad-scale voter discontent and civil unrest when the state can't be relied upon to provide basic services and/or deliver broad economic growth. And poverty isn't just a problem 'over there' anymore—wealth gaps are on the rise in the United States of America, Canada, France, Sweden and Germany (among others), and we've been forced to coin new terms (such as 'working poor') to cope with the stark reality that, for ever-growing numbers of people, having a job isn't always enough to put food on the table. Likewise, people from poorer countries are increasingly packing up the few belongings they have and 'voting with their feet', journeying to richer countries to seek a better life (whether by choice or necessity).

Cheap internet access makes it easier than ever for poor migrants to peer into the lives of those more fortunate than they are and to glimpse the promise of a higher standard of living. What's more, cheap global travel means that they don't need to spend their whole lives on the outside, looking in. The end of the rainbow, with its promised pot of gold, has never been more within reach. Increasingly, too, poor migrants are tech-savvy travelers, armed with potent tools such as smartphones and Facebook. In fact, many organizations aiding refugees often report that the first question that migrants ask when crossing a border is: "What is the Wi-Fi password?"

THE STARTING POINT FOR THIS BOOK is the recognition of our collective failure to adequately translate decades of good intentions and earnest efforts into complete and lasting global poverty elimination. For all our intellectual advances, for all our technological innovations, foreign aid budgets, impact assessment studies, tools, methodologies, data, symposia, campaigns and benefit rock concerts: half the world's population lives in poverty, and up to a quarter of these live in extreme poverty. To point out this collective failure is not, I think, a controversial thing to do. The poor are still with us, and on our current trajectory, they always will be.

Against this backdrop, I offer a deceptively simple question: *who owns poverty?* It's certainly not an idea we've ever articulated before—although, if you re-examine development thinking and practice through the lens of this startling question, you might conclude we had quite strong feelings on the subject all along.

Global poverty discourse has, to date, concerned itself with the question: *what is poverty?* This seems reasonable, given that good poverty solutions depend on good poverty definitions. Yet there's also something subtler at work here, when you consider that owning a thing starts with naming it. Adam named the beasts in the field and the fowl in the air. Conquistadors (re)named the lands they 'discovered' on behalf of their sovereigns. We name stars, diseases and social trends in order to bring them into our sphere of influence. We name, we claim.

When it comes to who has naming power over global poverty, it is almost too obvious (to the point of embarrassment) to point out that poor people have traditionally been relegated to a non-speaking part in someone else's narrative about their lives. They are passive recipients of someone else's poverty definition, someone else's poverty measurement. As a consequence of this, poor people are also locked out of the room where decisions get made about what our poverty solutions look like, unable to articulate their perspectives and priorities.

The question 'who owns poverty?' isn't one I pulled out of thin air. There was no 'eureka moment'. Rather, it emerged slowly, over the course of years, as a reaction to a number of things about the global poverty agenda that I found very puzzling indeed.

The initial seed of doubt was sewn with the realization that the definition of 'poor person' used by poverty experts rarely seemed to line up with what we were seeing in our work as a Foundation supporting microentrepreneurs in Paraguay (*Fundación Paraguaya*). Or rather, it didn't describe *everything* about them. The joy, generosity, creativity, problem-solving and entrepreneurial spirit we saw led us to conclude that the people we worked with were so much more than simply a binary classification of poor versus non-poor. Their lives were bigger than whether they lived on $1 per day or $2 per day. Those labels seemed all the more inapt and reductionist when applied to two people whose individual experiences of poverty differed completely from each other.

The next seed was one of discontent with the absurdity of there being so much poverty data in the world—but none that served the needs of poor people themselves. We take it for granted that the government departments and development organizations working to reduce poverty need poverty data to make good strategic and operational decisions. But rarely, if ever, do poverty experts consider poor people as equally important decision-makers, despite the fact that every day they solve problems related to their family's well-being.

7

As a result – in addition to having no input on what's being measured, how and when – poor people have no access to information collected about their lives and no control over what gets done with it, or by whom.

There are exceptions; I can point to a few promising initiatives that are 'listening to the voices of the poor' through participatory data collection and qualitative research. I wonder, however, whether we're only listening to what we want to hear (feedback on our own indicators, using our own process). I also wonder what happens to the insights generated through this listening. Are they used as a foundation to co-create and co-implement community-led development projects? Or are they simply used to tweak around the edges of our own standardized package of programs and services?

More typically, however, the anti-poverty program-design cycle starts with poverty experts descending on a village with clipboards, extracting pre-defined data points about the lives and livelihoods of poor people and returning to head office to aggregate the data into a spreadsheet. In the worst cases, it starts with consulting governments and civil servants rather than communities—as absurd a scenario as a doctor who takes the temperature of a hospital administrator, instead of the patient, before prescribing the medicine (in the words of my colleague, Andy Carrizosa).

The questions that the Foundation began asking were: What would happen if we gave poverty back to poor people? What would happen if we could find a way for poor people to ask their own questions and create their own poverty indicators? What if we could collect poverty information in a way that put relevant data into the hands of families, so they could be the ones planning and implementing their own family poverty-elimination program? And what if we allowed poor people to define what success looks like?

Over the past decade, the Foundation has been on a journey to do just that. While this journey is still underway, it is already signposted with a number of interesting landmarks and discoveries.

The first of these is that the richness of poverty can be found in its nuance. Thanks to the work of social scientists and economists in the Global North, we have a huge range of poverty indicators at our disposal. However, we have found that no single constellation of deprivations can be used to describe everyone's poverty. No single index can adequately capture the diverse ways in which a single family experiences poverty and non-poverty. If you believed Tolstoy when he said happy families are all alike, believe me when I say poor families are all poor in their own ways.

The second discovery relates to efficacy. When people have the power to name their own poverty, to call out their problems for themselves, they also have the power to do something about those problems. To define the solution; to own the solution. Time and again, we have seen poor families devising solutions to problems we previously considered intractable. And I'm not talking about solutions to *reduce* their poverty, or to *alleviate its effects* so as to make it a little more bearable, but solutions to *eliminate* their poverty once and for all.

What's more, we have seen poor families connecting to each other to share poverty solutions and ideas, rather than sourcing them from external aid workers. After all, not every individual in a community suffers from malnutrition. Not every individual in a community suffers from domestic violence. Where a poor person can identify someone else beating the odds in one particular aspect of poverty, they can create horizontal learning networks that tap into locally held knowledge and solutions. The poor can help not only themselves but also each other to overcome their deprivations.

We might have started with a small question, but what we've ended up with is nothing short of a revolution. This book is a first attempt to tell the story of that revolution.

As you read on, you'll also find a second revolution unfolding. While most of this story concerns the question of who owns poverty, a quieter question at play is: *who owns the global poverty agenda?* To date, that agenda has predominantly been the domain of thinkers and doers in the Global North, articulated and driven largely without meaningful input from thinkers and doers in the Global South. If we're going to eliminate poverty once and for all, we must give everyone a seat at the table; otherwise, we're missing out on a lot of potential insights and experiences that can meaningfully inform our collective work.

There's a particular tyranny associated with being from Paraguay. No one knows where it is, no one knows anything about it and (especially when you're in a room full of global poverty experts) no one seriously believes they have anything to learn from someone born there. I recall my boredom during countless networking sessions of countless international conferences when no one wanted to talk to 'that guy from Paraguay'. During these times, I found company in the form of 'that guy from Bangladesh'; he was doing the same conference circuit and feeling similarly overlooked by most everyone there. To escape the oppression of our insignificance, we once hopped into a taxi to tour whatever city we happened to be in at the time. That was before the world noticed he was doing amazing work—and before that work garnered him the Nobel Peace Prize.

For me, therefore, this book represents another important step toward ensuring that Southern voices are heard; toward finally integrating our perspectives, experiences and insights about the very pressing problem of global poverty (which is, after all, right outside our front door). And, to be honest, I'm not even talking about my perspective—because, in my own country, I come from a place of relative privilege. I'm talking about the real experts on poverty: people living in poverty.

The intellectual agenda, as articulated by the North, has carried us so far—but not far enough. Correctly, it has identified that the machine of poverty has a lot of moving parts. However, the solutions offered by the developmental industrial complex don't come equipped with a corresponding number of moving parts. At best, they're ineffective. At worst, they make the problem more acute. What's more, they do nothing to identify the poverty living in the rich man's house (because poverty isn't just confined to so-called 'poor countries').

This book offers a new framework and a promising approach, conceived and developed in Paraguay but as applicable in Angola as it is in Austria and Alabama. This radical new methodology corrects the shortcomings of the current paradigm by putting poor families at the center of the conversation about what it means to be poor, what it means to be not poor and how to get from one to the other.

The pages that follow chart a journey in progress, and there will be times when I offer more questions than answers. For this, I cannot apologize. Asking 'who owns poverty?' has fundamentally changed the kinds of conversations I have about poverty and has positively changed the work we do as an organization. My aim is to encourage more people, and more development organizations, to ask themselves this very same question—and find the answers that will help them do more meaningful, more engaged, more sustainable and, ultimately, more impactful work.

I WROTE THIS BOOK for people who are frustrated with current global and national anti-poverty efforts and are searching for a new approach to eliminating poverty. People who believe all human beings, no matter how poor, can lift themselves out of poverty in this generation through self-help, encouragement, mentoring and compassionate support. People who believe in self-reliance as a liberating experience

11

for everyone involved. People who know we are all poor in some ways and rich in others, and that this common vulnerability allows us to dispense with unhelpful turns of phrase, such as 'the haves and have-nots'. It's no longer a question of 'us versus them'. Winning the war against global poverty requires us to discover our oneness.

I bring to this book more than three decades of experience in working with and for the poor in many parts of the world. This work began in Paraguay and, over time, found a home in countries across the world, including Taiwan, England, the U.S., Tanzania, Nigeria, Argentina, Mexico, Ecuador, Colombia, Bolivia, Chile, Brazil, Papua New Guinea, Singapore, Malaysia and South Africa. My journey of trying to improve social justice has not been without disappointment and excitement as I learned about my limitations and grew with my successes and failures.

I have been lucky to always understand, just like Bernard of Chartres in the 12th century, *nanos gigantum humeris insidentes*—that I have been a dwarf standing on the shoulders of giants. As I have climbed the rungs of my ladder, leaning on different walls over time, I have been able to appreciate those who came before me: the thinkers, fighters, dreamers, poets, stubborn leaders—anyone and everyone who never relented in their fight for a fairer world.

CHAPTER 1
GALA DINNER

"WHO PAID FOR this gala dinner?" Our high school, even in its fifth year, was struggling to cover its operational costs—so I was more than a little taken aback by the extravagance of the scene underway before us. I turned to Luis Fernando Sanabria, a trusted friend and colleague whose candor I had come to rely on over the years, but instead of answering he just turned to me and smiled.

It was December 2008. The summer evening was hot and muggy; the familiar cries of toucans and parakeets competed with *Pomp and Circumstance* playing on the loudspeaker. Diplomas in hand, smartly capped and gowned, our proud graduates marched single-file out of the campus chapel. There, they were met by an outdoor banquet, furtively laid during the ceremony by the second-year students. The courtyard stood transformed, flecked with tables topped with white tablecloths and floral centerpieces, under the welcome shade of the tall mango tree. Parents and students mingled, laughing and snapping pictures of each other. A bell rang and suddenly the graduates melted away, without a word, into a nearby classroom block. They re-emerged some minutes later dressed for a ball, the girls elegantly turned out in matching pink gowns, the boys boasting suits and ties.

If you hadn't known we were in the middle of one of the poorest regions of rural Paraguay, the graduation ceremony might have comfortably passed for one in the capital city. For our graduates, it was a way to surprise their parents—poor subsistence farmers with little or no formal education, for whom even the disposable plastic tablecloths, paper plates and cups represented unimaginable opulence.

Before they had arrived at the Cerrito Agricultural High School, this was the life our students knew, too: waking at four in the morning to work the family farm, cultivating ten acres using only hand tools, planting one crop to eat and one to sell for the cash needed to buy other staples. Going to town meant a six-mile walk. Selling at market was a rare occasion. Formal education consisted of two hours of travel for a three-hour school day, sandwiched in between morning and evening chores on the farm. To say that these families earn one or two dollars per person per day implies a level and predictable income over the course of the year, but in reality, a farmer's income is lumpy and seasonal. Money comes in at harvest time and, with any luck, lasts until the next one. Many times, it doesn't.

Life was even harsher for our students from indigenous *Guaraní* tribes. The *Guaraní* make up 2 percent of the county's population, but they barely register by other standards. As traditional hunters and farmers, they weren't integrated into the market economy and, with the privatization of land ownership, their traditional hunting and farming lands swiftly disappeared. By and large, the *Guaraní* were moved to government reservations and expected to take up subsistence farming—in the poorest lands, in the most remote areas, with 'separate but equal' education and health care that was anything but 'equal'. Extreme poverty was a daily and inescapable reality.

I surveyed the scene from the safety of the chapel steps. To my left stood the local Catholic bishop who had celebrated mass before the graduation ceremony. To my right stood Jorge Guerrero, a recent graduate who had been invited to play guitar during the ceremony, and Luis Fernando, my Chief Operating Officer and *confidant*. We stood in silence, but my heart pounded with confusion and doubt.

Our little experiment had only recently hit the break-even point, five years in. Yes—we'd finally cracked the nut on how to make agricultural education pay for itself. But that didn't mean we weren't still counting every last penny. Who had approved the funds for this party, and why hadn't I been told? What was wrong with the ceremony we had last year? It wasn't fancy, but everyone enjoys a typical *campesino* hog roast in a rustic barn, right? Was this where our school was headed? Once we have enough cash we'll splash out on silly proms?

Luis Fernando finally spoke: "Relax. The students paid for this *fiesta* with the money they saved from running the campus grocery store. They all bought cell phones ages ago, and they decided they wanted to do something nice for their parents."

On the face of things, what he was saying made sense. The whole scene was a striking testament to just how far the students had come. It wasn't simply a measure of distance (although perhaps you could see it in that light; for many parents, the journey to the school would have involved walking for hours down red dirt roads to reach the nearest public transportation, eight hours to the central bus terminal in Asunción and another few hours on a bus to the school)—it was a measure of their transformation. Three years ago, these poor students arrived at our boarding school with barely enough clothes to cover their backs. Many were thin and malnourished. Most could not read or write above a fifth-grade level, although they had all completed ninth grade at their public schools. And yet, here they were: newly mint-ed high-school graduates. They were bright, confident and capable—and looking quite at ease in the regalia of the middle class.

At the very least, I was reassured to hear the school wasn't footing the bill for the party. We needed to keep our academ-ic and operational costs to a minimum so our school could be financially self-sufficient. However, we also encouraged students to run their own cooperative business on campus: a little grocery store stocking snacks, toiletries, stationery and other essentials. They kept all the profits they earned and, of course, we let them choose how to spend their money.

For all my doubts, I trusted that Luis Fernando was telling me the truth. We had worked together for almost 20 years. Short, athletic, with piercing black eyes, he earned the respect of all who knew him with his incisive comments and ability to see beyond the obvious. He was a person of rare qualities: Born into a middle-class Paraguayan family, he attended a vocational high school and worked to pay his way through law school. Thanks to his work ethic and enviable capacity for team building, he had occupied almost every position in our organization, until the Board and I decided to name him Chief Operating Officer. In this role, he oversaw the day-to-day operations of our microfinance and youth-entrepreneurship education programs, as well as our agricul-tural school. If anyone had a finger on the school's pulse, it was Luis Fernando.

Yet I still couldn't understand why our students had cho-sen to spend their hard-earned cash on some fancy dinner. We were preparing them for an austere life of hard work on the farm, which made the extravagance of the evening all the more baffling. And what kind of example were we setting for them by allowing to this happen? I shook my head in disbelief.

As Luis Fernando started down the steps to join the crowd, he glanced up and added: "It's nice for the parents, isn't it? Besides, most of the students have been accepted into college, and they wanted to celebrate."

I nearly fell over.

Jorge must have seen the shock on my face. "He's right," he offered. "Once we come here, we don't want to return to the farm right away. We're not ready. We get bitten by the city bug, and we want to go to college. There's nothing going on back home—we don't even get a good cellphone signal there."

Jorge's constant smile betrayed not even a hint of his difficult upbringing. He was born into a large family of farmers living in extreme poverty. Although their farm was productive, there were so many mouths to feed that it failed to keep them above the poverty line. Every child, even the youngest, had their own daily chores in the home and on the farm. The house, although always tidy, was small and cramped. Its walls were made of mud, board and plastic sheets; the roof of tin. His mother and sisters prepared their food on the rammed-earth kitchen floor beside an open fire, whose smoke invaded every room. Despite all the hardships they faced, Jorge's parents placed a high value on education and sent all of their children to school—even the girls. Together they were a kind, loyal and generous family, poor in some ways and rich in more ways than one.

As I turned to Jorge, I couldn't help but notice the sleek cell phone tucked into his shirt pocket. He had been one of the most diligent students in his class and, by all appearances, he was doing well for himself. "Nice to have you back on campus. What are you up to these days?"

"I'm halfway through the National University's six-year agronomy program. I am living at an old-age home run by the Ministry of Health—when I arrived, I convinced them to let me manage the vegetable garden in exchange for room and board. It was funny—they'd never even thought of running their garden as a business, and they were really impressed when I brought them the numbers. It's doing really well; I even bought myself a small laptop computer and a cell phone." He tapped his shirt pocket.

I smiled to myself. *Technology is changing everything.* Cell phones had gone from being a luxury item for the middle class to a staple for just about everyone, even me. In fact, cell phones were soon to become not just a personal accessory but a professional necessity—the backbone of our work with poor communities. But on that day, had you told me I'd soon team up with Hewlett-Packard to create a platform that poor families could use to self-diagnose their poverty on just such a 'pocket computer', I'd have laughed at you.

In that moment, however, my thoughts were on Jorge— a former student who was clearly full of the same sort of aspiration on display among the graduating class. Was this really what our school was about? Teaching peasants to mimic the middle class?

I turned and studied the bishop's face for any hint of what he might have been thinking. Paraguay was, and still is, a nation of Catholics. As the head of the local diocese, he was a figure of authority with a great deal of influence in the community. What he thought mattered. A lot.

On the surface, all was going well for our institution. Our graduates were obviously thriving, and our school had broken even a few months before. Our radical plan had worked: we had transformed a bankrupt agricultural school into a financially self-sufficient one that covered its costs through the production and sale of vegetables, chicken, eggs and pork. Not only that, but we had converted an old dormitory block into a small (but profitable) rural hotel, and we sold technical assistance to organizations that wanted to replicate our educational model in other countries.

But to my mind, there were two things going on here that were out of sync with our original model. Our school was always meant to be an austere technical-vocational program for young farmers living in extreme poverty. The assumption was that our graduating students would take their new skills and knowledge back to the family farm, and help their parents to improve their land and their yield. By turning farmers into *better* farmers we thought we could prevent, or at least ameliorate, the massive rural–urban migration underway in the country. Paraguay's agricultural sector may have been modernizing, thanks to the influx of money from direct foreign investment and loans from the World Bank and other private investors, but most of this investment flowed to big agribusiness—the majority of subsistence farmers were being left behind.

Now, here were our students: celebrating three years of hard work and achievement with a pointless waste of money. Rather than looking ahead to their lives as farmers, they were pretending to be young professionals of the country's nascent middle class. And on top of that, most of them preferred to go on to university than return home. Why on earth were we teaching them about agriculture if they were just going to move to the city? Were we wasting our money? Were we un-wittingly making the problem of rural flight worse? I voiced my concerns to the bishop.

"I also sometimes grapple with these questions," he began. "But remember that things have changed in our country. In the early sixties, I was sent to a rural village to live among poor peasants. Back then, many poor farmers and their families suffered from ignorance, isolation and malnutrition. One of my first tasks was to teach them how to cook the most basic meals and to diversify their diet with what they could grow in their homes. We also organized farmers into cooperatives, so they could pool resources and collectively demand better prices from buyers. Not that the

dictator always looked kindly on this, but that's another story. Like you, we wanted farmers to have a decent life. But it's
a hard life, and I can understand when rural youth reject it.
But I also suffer when I see young farmers buy motorcycles
and cell phones. You see, the Church makes a distinction
between misery and poverty. We don't like misery, as it di-
minishes human beings as God's creation. We think it is a
sin for poor people not to want to improve their lot. There
are three types of love – love for God, love for thy neighbor
and love for thyself – but we don't think that poverty is all
that wrong. On the contrary, poverty can be a positive thing,
when it means rejecting unnecessary material things and
leading a purposeful life, rather than turning into mindless
consumers."

With that, and a shrug, he turned to leave. He looked
tired. He never discussed it, but he obviously led a difficult
life under the military dictatorship. Organizing peasants
into self-help groups to demand their political and economic
rights was a dangerous occupation. But more than that, the
message of simplicity and austerity that the Church promoted seemed increasingly out of step with the way the country
was moving. The very materialism he preached against was
taking firm root in Paraguayan society. The more you owned,
the happier you were—austerity was going out of style. As he
walked away, I noticed that he, too, had a cell phone in his
back pocket.

It wasn't my first, and definitely wasn't to be my last,
conversation with the Catholic Church about the idea of
poverty. In fact, the Church would be a constant presence in
our work in Paraguay. Years later, I would even find myself
in the Vatican, meeting with the Pope and other Church
leaders to discuss the work of the Foundation. In many ways,
the Church was a perfect microcosm of the broader debate
on poverty. For example, it fully embraced the challenge of
listening to the voices of the poor and creating a more equal

and peaceful society. Opinion was divided, however, about whether overcoming poverty was actually possible. Many cleaved to the traditional view that 'the poor shall always be with you', in stark contrast to those (especially in Latin America in the fifties and sixties) whose reaction to widespread social injustice was to preach a more Marxist-leaning 'liberation theology'.

I found Luis Fernando in the crowd and recounted my conversation with the bishop. "These students may be poor, but they are not stupid, Martín," he responded. "They have been exposed to a different reality here in school and they don't want to go back home to subsistence farming. Most of them have participated in our youth-entrepreneurship programs and have met hundreds of students from other parts of the country—sometimes at formal dinners such as this one. They don't want to be poor peasants like their parents. They see the value of education, and they know they can make a living with their skills. Most of them may not be returning to their family farms directly, but they will surely find good jobs in the city and attend college at night. And in the end, they will bring more resources and wealth to their families. Now come sit down—the waltz is about to start. The girls will dance with their fathers and the boys with their mothers. Then there will be rock and salsa."

I looked at him in amazement. Don't get me wrong: there was no doubt that I was proud of our students. I was proud of what they'd achieved in their time at our school. I was also proud of my team, who worked hard to make this school the very place where the students could thrive. *And yet.*

Nothing in my life had prepared me for what I saw on the dance floor that day—seeing poor peasants transformed into something else. At that point, I had spent over thirty years thinking about poverty, working to reduce poverty and convincing others to join the fight. My work came in many guises; I had been a student, a mayor, a professor,

21

an international trade negotiator and the head of the Foundation. Those many years had taught me that poverty was a complex beast. Poverty was difficult to alleviate. And, most of all, it wasn't at all easy to say what poverty actually was. It had something to do with what was happening with the national economy: with investment frameworks and the balance of trade and oil prices and foreign wars. It had something to do with the look of apathy on the face of a poor farmer who, when he is not harvesting, sits in front of his house doing nothing. It had something to do with bad roads, and floods, and crop failure. It had something to do with education, and quite a lot to do with expectations and aspirations: whether you knew a better life awaited you, and whether it was anyone's job but your own to make sure you achieved it. *And yet.*

I thought of Jorge when he first arrived at our school. He was so intimidated by his new surroundings and my staff that he couldn't even look you in the eye when you spoke to him; his gaze would remain firmly fixed on the floor, and he struggled to speak above a mumble. Three years later, that same boy had the guts to do something unheard of: negotiate his room and board with the Ministry of Health using the very skills he'd learned at our school. What was that, if not a story of a young man climbing his way of out poverty? *And yet.*

Let's assume, for a moment, that somehow our school was helping these kids to not only climb but *fly* their way out of poverty. How had it happened so quickly? Three years didn't seem long enough for such a metamorphosis. Through the Foundation's microfinance program, we'd been working with some clients for twice that time—and while some of them had improved, many of them remained stagnant. Perhaps, because of this, we had come to believe that, despite our best efforts, not everyone was going to make it out of poverty. Maybe we thought that the best we could hope for was to make things a little bit better for most the people we served. *And yet…*

Let's assume, for a moment, that our students really were transformed—on the cusp of joining the middle class and making their own way in the world. Was this kind of transformation even desirable? Were we doing the right thing, sending them far away from their families with no discernible safety net? *Pygmalion* was a nice fairytale, but was a happy ending in store for our real-life Eliza Doolittles? No one could predict whether the middle class would welcome, with open arms, these young people with their different accents, different ways of dressing and eating, and different life stories. What is the point of opening up a middle-class factory if our students would be ostracized and ghettoized once they got to the city? And just who would be left in the countryside to do the farming? Were we doing more harm than good without even knowing it?

As *The Blue Danube* poured out from the loudspeakers and the eyes of the crowd turned to the dance floor, I suddenly remembered something. *This wasn't the first time I'd seen this transformation.*

CHAPTER 2
THE PLAGUE

M Y HEART WAS IN my throat as I ascended the steps
of the National Development Bank in downtown
Asunción in May 1985. It was a building designed to intim-
idate: a neoclassical fortress with oversized brass doors and
a huge neon sign on the roof that read 'Stroessner: Peace
and Progress'—an unsubtle reminder from our dictator that
he had the best interests of the country at heart. Not that
this political branding exercise rang true for the average
Paraguayan in those days. 'Peace' was achieved through a
repressive regime that suspended civil liberties and tortured,
killed or exiled its opponents; 'progress' meant being elite
enough to be on the receiving end of state largesse, or com-
pliant enough to be allowed access to basic services.

Located in south-central South America, Paraguay is a
small landlocked country roughly the size of California, but
with only a tenth of its population. Compared to the Latin
American average of the day, Paraguay was poor in most
economic and social indicators. Wars with its neighbors, a
protracted civil war and a string of brutal dictatorships had
left the country with neither a functioning civil society nor
rule of law—and its powerful neighbors, Argentina and
Brazil, utterly took advantage of it. Needless to say, it was

not a country ripe with opportunity for the vast majority of its population. By 1985, two-thirds of its inhabitants lived in rural areas, gross national product (GNP) per capita was only $950, half the workforce was outside the formal sector and hundreds of thousands of Paraguayans had fled abroad to find work. Paraguayan children were ten times as likely to die before their fifth birthday as children in the US, and the average life span was only 67 years. Poverty was rampant, a fact that was well-understood despite there being no official statistics on the matter.

I was thrown into that world of extreme poverty during my year of compulsory military service in 1975. Fresh out of my Jesuit high-school education (under the tutelage of priests preaching a seditious brand of liberation theology across the country), I left for an army base in the wild, semi-arid Chaco near the Bolivian border—a vast, sparsely populated and desperately poor region of the country. The journey there could be measured in hundreds of miles from the capital, but it was thousands of miles from the comfortable middle-class life I had known until that point.

Many of my fellow soldiers were born and raised in poor rural communities and had never set foot in the capital. I soon learned I was the only member of my unit who had graduated from high school, one of only a few who knew how to read and write, the only one who owned a toothbrush (it caused considerable tension with my fellow soldiers that I was unwilling to share it with them). Because I had played rugby in school, I was lucky to be in relatively good physical shape, which meant I escaped the harsh punishment meted out to whoever couldn't complete our grueling training exercises.

As I adjusted to my new environment, I swore to myself that the dictator could claim my service, but he would never claim my body and mind. Surviving meant staying in shape, obeying orders without question and keeping my opinions to myself—even when it meant seeing political prisoners my own age too broken by years of torture to pose any credible threat to the government (if indeed they ever had). Difficult as it might have been at the time, I am grateful for that year of my life because it revealed the unvarnished truth about the political and economic reality of my country—an experience that only strengthened my resolve to work toward building a more just society when I left.

By that time, General Stroessner's regime had destroyed two generations of lives in my country, and my family was no exception. My grandmother was a notable leader in the women's rights and anti-fascist movements; my father was one of the Co-Founders of a prominent bilingual school and a visible member of the opposition. Their outspoken criticism of the regime had led them to be blacklisted, and life was difficult for them in so many ways. Yet despite being persecuted (or perhaps because of it), they instilled in me a sense of civic responsibility that has shaped my own determination to work on behalf of those less fortunate than me. Still, my time in the army had taught me what Stroessner was capable of, and I knew real social change wouldn't be possible without political regime change. I also knew he couldn't stay in power forever—and, until then, I could prepare myself to be part of the next chapter of our country's history. The question, of course, was figuring out how.

Many of my fellow high-school students had embraced the teaching of the Jesuit priests—a world in which liberation theology became a dream of overthrowing the regime through a Marxist uprising (similar to those underway elsewhere in Latin America). While this vision of the poor inheriting our beautiful country may have been seductive, my father cautioned me against any measure of enthusiasm for replacing one brutal dictatorship with another. And so it was that, after graduation, I left for the army—and some of my friends in Asunción launched their own guerrilla movement.

By the time I came back, far too many of them had been arrested and tortured by the government, and a few had been exiled or killed. There was never any doubt in my mind that becoming involved in opposition politics could only lead to the same outcome for me. A net was swiftly closing over anyone else who had been involved with the Jesuits at the school, and I knew it was time for me to leave my country.

Armed with scholarships, I took up undergraduate studies in the United States, and graduate studies in Spain: studying public administration, economics, science and technology, and national development planning—four subjects I believed would help my country's development effort. My time in the US was instructive in other ways as well. I learned to appreciate its varied culture, its democratic values, its tolerance to different ideas and its capacity to compromise. Like other Latin Americans, I was amazed at how everything in the US seemed to work so well: its highways, its social safety net, its space program. I returned to Paraguay aged 28 and newly married to my college sweetheart, Dorothy, who would become my life-long companion, trusted advisor and mother of our three beautiful children.

My first job was at the Ministry of Industry and Commerce, where I was promptly tasked with drafting a new national biofuel plan. Paraguay had an ample supply of sugar cane, and its supplies of cheap labor were just as plentiful. By turning sugar cane into ethanol, we could substitute our oil imports and boost the national economy at the same time. The plan hinged on foreign private investors bringing technology and managerial know-how, the government providing soft loans, the state-owned petroleum company being required to add ethanol to gasoline, and price-fixing to guarantee profits all around. Students of Latin American economic history will recall that the prevailing illusion at the time was that the only way to kick-start widespread economic development was with planned government interventions—a far cry from the dominant neoliberal paradigm we know so well today. In reality, the biofuel plan would have only benefited those with government connections, lining the pockets of the few at the expense of the many. But it wasn't my job to criticize. It was my job to do as I was told. So I drafted and presented the biofuel plan.

And then I was fired.

I'd like to point out that my sudden lack of employment had absolutely nothing to do with the quality of my work. Rather, it was because I refused to join the ruling Colorado Party, the civilian backbone of the dictatorship. I may have been caught off-guard by this turn of events, but I was far from surprised. I knew very well that my family's opposition to the regime rendered me unacceptable to them. So, black-listed – as were my parents, my grandparents, and hundreds of thousands of others before me – I was unable to find a job in government. The problem was, I had specialized in national development planning. What use would these skills be if I couldn't work at the national level? The only other option was to work in the private sector, but I couldn't see myself doing that. I wanted to do purposeful and meaningful work that had an impact on the lives of the poor. Yet there was simply no middle road at the time; civil society organizations were non-existent, save a tiny handful of charities that raised money for orphans and the blind.

I landed on what seemed like a promising notion: starting my own organization to work directly with poor and excluded communities. Focusing on political issues was out of the question; instead, I would help people expand their economic opportunities. I turned the streets of Asunción into my research lab, talking to as many poor street vendors as I could find. In doing so, it became clear that the two critical gaps they faced (beyond, obviously, their lack of political voice and representation) were the lack of business skills and affordable credit they needed to make a decent living.

I assembled a group of friends and – with much support from (among others) my brother Esteban and his law firm partner Guillermo Peroni, other local businessmen and a US-based non-profit called Accion International – in February of 1985 we created the country's first modern, non-charitable development organization: *Fundación Paraguaya de Cooperación y Desarrollo* (the Paraguay Foundation of Cooperation and Development). Our mission was to provide loans and business training so that microenterprises in the informal economic sector could increase their family income, strengthen their precarious jobs and create new jobs. While the Foundation was notable for being the first development NGO in the country, for me personally it marked another important turning point. I had moved from one extreme of the economic development spectrum to the other—from working on the wealth of the nation to the wealth of its nationals; from macro to micro.

Microenterprise development itself was nothing new: credit and savings schemes for microenterprises had been popping up across Latin America and the world for years, based on the idea that poor people were economic agents rather than charity cases. The radical idea was that bottom-up economic development could work—if only we viewed urban street vendors, shopkeepers, home-based carpenters and seamstresses, and rural subsistence farmers as an opportunity for economic growth and poverty reduction, rather than a burden to society. With access to credit and training, these very small businesses would be capable of not only increasing their income, strengthening precarious jobs and creating new ones but also 'graduating' into the formal, tax-paying economy.

It was an idea whose time had come. Starting in the early 1980s, major international and regional development agencies across the world began handing out grants to these new microenterprise development programs. For Latin America, microenterprise development was a response to our 'lost decade'. As traditional modernization, import substitution, industrialization, credit subsidization and top-down government development schemes (like my national biofuel plan) ran out of steam – because of a heavy foreign debt burden, stifling bureaucracy and untenable national development plans – international development agencies began searching for new strategies. Microenterprise development was seen as a fresh, new, market-oriented strategy to combat poverty through job creation—in this case, self-employment. It viewed the entrepreneur, rather than the state, as the engine of economic development. Private-sector job creation was the new darling, and donor funding started flowing like water.

The novelty of what we were proposing, however, was that the Foundation would deliver financial services and managerial training without relying on grants from donors to cover our operational costs in the long term. We were going to help poor people become financially self-sufficient rather than reliant on charity—and we would do it by creating a financially self-sufficient organization that didn't rely on the charity of donors.

Our business plan was ambitious, laying out a three-year strategy to break even. To help us get there, USAID gave us a tiny start-up grant to cover some of our operational costs. To keep us focused on sustainability (and help us prove our credibility), the local USAID Director, Paul Fritz, insisted we source our initial loan capital from a local institution. A small loan from the Inter-American Development Bank was on its way, but wouldn't arrive soon enough. For this reason, I made my way to the National Development Bank, on the other side of those huge brass doors in downtown Asunción, in May 1985.

THE BANK MANAGER scrutinized me from the other side of his desk as he thumbed through my loan application for $50,000. His tall, stout frame was draped in a shiny gray suit and a red tie; his mustache was finely clipped. The red lapel pin on his suit, with a little white star in the middle, affirmed his loyalty to the government's political party. Finally, he spoke. "I thought you said that you were going to support small industries. But here I see that although you do intend to support a few micro-industries, your focus will be to support microenterprises, including street vendors. I don't understand."

I had anticipated these concerns, and quickly placed a copy of our just-completed business plan on his desk. "Our market study shows that microenterprises create as many or even more jobs than micro-industries," I assured him. "We know that by supporting the informal sector we can help these small shop owners and street vendors increase their family income, strengthen their precarious jobs and even create new jobs. Eventually, they will become formal businesses."

"I think you came to the wrong bank," he patiently intoned. "We are a development bank. Do you understand?" He then proceeded to lecture me about the stages of economic growth; how the bank served the country's five-year national development plan; how import substitution, exports and industrialization were the key to national progress; how trickle-down economics would transform the country. He couldn't have been more condescending had he drawn it in crayon. Without pausing to draw breath, he continued: "These 'microenterprises', as you call them, don't contribute to our country's gross national product. They are too small, too insignificant. We need real jobs, not under-employed people."

This was a surprise. I had expected him to be conservative—but not aggressive. Hoping to reassure him we were on

31

the same side, I changed tack. "Of course, industrialization and adding value to our exports is the way to go for our country overall. But our aim is to work with poor men and women who aren't skilled enough to get jobs at those factories. They can't read; they can't even fill out a job application. They are chronically unemployed and we want to give them a hand." Sensing his continued resistance, I added: "Maybe – definitely – after a few years of support some of these microenterprises will join the formal sector, pay taxes and grow to become small industries."

"I doubt it very much," he responded. "I don't know where you get your ideas, but they are very naïve. The bank's strategy – the country's strategy – is not just something we made up out of thin air. It has been drafted with the help of dozens of international experts from the Inter-American Development Bank, the World Bank and the UN. Even USAID has always supported our strategy, so I don't know why they are even considering this nonsense about street vendors."

I realized my loan application was being rejected then and there. The interview hadn't lasted more than 30 minutes. I was dumbfounded that his faith in the state's power over the economy had made him so blind to what was happening outside his very door. In my desperation, I pointed out the window toward the tiny market stalls lining the plaza below. "So what will you do about these informal workers? The national development plan doesn't mention anything about them. Nobody mentions them. They aren't just farmers who can wait an eternity on their rural farms doing subsistence agriculture until the country gets richer and their lives improve. These are people who came from the countryside a long time ago and who live in the slums by the river. They are barely surviving—even starving. Don't you think they need support from the state, or at least from society?"

He didn't hesitate. "Personally, I believe that street vendors are the plague. Don't quote me. They are everywhere, but where are they coming from? No one knows, but they don't pay taxes and they don't contribute to the economy. We need to exterminate them, to get rid of them. They embarrass our country and they don't make our capital city look good for the tourists. Don't get me wrong, I don't mean exterminate them in the literal sense of killing them, but we should starve them out. If we give them loans, they will spread like the plague. If we deprive them of help, eventually they'll get tired of selling under the sun all day and they will give up."

To hear an educated government official refer to poor people in such callous terms shocked me. It was the first time I'd heard such anti-poor rhetoric coming out of the mouth of officialdom. Needless to say, it wouldn't be the last; nor would it be the only variation on the theme. One variation – lectured at me time and again by Paraguayan government economists and bureaucrats – was that I shouldn't question state development policy, which had been articulated by reputable international development agencies such as the World Bank, the Inter-American Development Bank and USAID. (The message here: They know better than us. Local solutions to local problems need not apply. If poor countries knew how to fix themselves, they would have done it already.)

The second variation was that we should be focusing on the wealth of nations, rather than the well-being of specific individuals within those nations. (Read: Poverty has nothing to do with poor people.) As we now know, however, wealth creation at a national level doesn't automatically translate into wealth for everyone in society. The third variation was that poor people don't know what is good for them, otherwise they wouldn't be poor (the Protestant work ethic writ large).

I left the National Development Bank acutely aware that I was swimming upstream against the strong current of thinking around what poverty is—and what we can and should do about it. But to my mind, working with poor people to increase their income was an inherently worthwhile thing to do, as was building a financially sustainable pro-poor Foundation. We would support income generation by providing the financial services that microentrepreneurs needed to manage their cashflow, invest, save and take advantage of market opportunities. And we would help them do all of this well by giving them free business-management training.

Our theory of change was simple: increasing incomes would lead to improved family well-being. It took two decades, one gala dinner and one secret beauty pageant in a slum for me to realize just how very wrong we were.

CHAPTER 3
CHAMELEONS AND CRABS

I SHOULD HAVE SEEN it coming. With the benefit of hindsight, the signs were clear all along, but in those early days I was too busy trying to obtain loan capital to take much notice of them. In the wake of my disastrous meeting with the Head of the National Development Bank, I pitched our business plan to a number of local commercial banks, with much the same result. Finally, I called an old family friend, Antonio Espinoza.

Antonio was a successful local businessman who had launched his own savings and loan bank. When he suggested I stop by his office that same afternoon, I practically ran the entire way across town. Once there, I didn't waste any time explaining my idea.

"With one loan from your bank, we can reach thousands of poor women with small, $20 microloans. I know this sounds crazy, but we know they can repay us. We know that because they're already borrowing from local loan sharks at extortionate rates—and if they borrow from us instead, they can use what they would have paid in interest to the loan shark and invest in their business, or set the money aside for a rainy day. They can increase their income, use that money to make their lives better in all sorts of ways. We know it works because it's happening all around the world. And not only that, we'll provide business-management courses at night in our offices—on topics such as basic accounting, inventory management, leadership, human resources, sales and other things they'll need to succeed. We've got a classroom and our training manuals are printed and ready to go. So what do you think?"

He considered my proposal and asked precisely the right question: "You say that you know that poor people can repay a loan, but how do you know that they will? If a poor person doesn't repay a loan shark, the loan shark shows up at their home or market stall and refuses to leave until he gets his money back. You want to reach thousands of people with only a handful of Loan Officers—how will you keep on top of all of those financial relationships?"

"We can do it by learning from international experience. We'll form 'solidarity groups' of people that all know each other, and can vouch for the character and credit-worthiness of their fellow group members. It's up to the group to make sure that everyone repays their loan, not the Loan Officer. But we'll also provide incentives: if everyone repays their $20 loan on time, they can apply for a $35 loan next time around, and so on."

This was a textbook response—right out of the universal microcredit playbook. That's not to say it was incorrect, but it was missing the broader point he was making about how much we really knew about what was going on in the lives of poor people. Microcredit is both a business and a personal relationship—and, by and large, it outsources the personal side of things to the group itself. The personal relationships between group members ensure that any challenges a client faces (illness, business failure, etc.) won't get in the way of them repaying their loan. And not getting involved in the finer details of our clients' lives meant the Foundation could stick to the business side of things, for maximum efficiency.

Thus, thanks to the loan from Antonio's bank (for which he became a personal guarantor before joining our Board for over 30 years), and a few more from other local banks once we'd 'proved' ourselves, the Foundation grew to the point where we could finance all our new loans from the interest earned on existing loans. We reached more and more clients, our clients were repaying their loans and everything seemed to be going smoothly. Soon, we even cracked the capital markets, issuing bonds on the local stock market (a first for the country, and maybe even the region). But in all of the excitement surrounding securing that initial bank loan and opening our doors for business, I missed spotting what was my first real-life lesson on poverty.

That lesson came in the shape of a middle-aged woman selling *chipas* on a street corner in downtown Asunción. For the uninitiated, *chipas* should be at the very top of your list of reasons to visit Paraguay; they are small, baked cheese corn-flour rolls, typically eaten as a midday snack, and they are wonderful. On our first day of business, I headed out into the city with our first Loan Officer. Armed with blank loan applications and unbridled enthusiasm, we were ready to find microentrepreneurs who wanted to apply for a small business loan and receive free business-management training.

That's when we met the *chipa* lady: a middle-aged woman with a smile no less dazzling for its missing teeth. She was perched on a stool on the pavement with a deep basket lined with a white sheet, which lifted to reveal some three-dozen warm *chipas* she peddled to passers-by. Surely this was the very picture of a microenterprise we wanted to serve?

I bought a few *chipas* for myself and my Loan Officer and, after a few minutes of small talk, I asked the woman some basic questions about her business—whether she baked her *chipas* herself or bought them from a supplier, how much she spent every day on supplies and what her typical daily turnover was.

She was surprisingly forthcoming. "I used to bake at home but I don't anymore. I have my mother to take care of. She is not doing so well, you know. She used to help me but not anymore. So, I take out a $20-dollar day loan from a man in the market near my home and from there I go to a woman's house where I buy 150 *chipas* every day. I load them in my basket and take a bus here every day—rain or shine. When I return home, I go to the market and pay the man his $20 plus $10 in daily interest. I keep the rest, which is not that much. The next day, the same thing. I can't tell you how many *chipas* I sell because every day is different. One day I sell a lot; the next day I sell less." She paused, sizing me up. "Why do you want to know all of this?"

I smiled and told her about our Foundation, that we wanted to provide loans and night classes to people like her. I explained that our loan sizes were based on cashflow, which was why I wanted to understand how much she sold every day.

"What you're asking is impossible. I could tell you that I sell 100 *chipas* a day, but I would be lying, because one day I can sell 90 and another day 110. But I never sell one hundred, so I can't tell you one hundred, because it would not be true," she said. "Tell me what you really want to know. Do you want me to tell you that I sell a lot, or a little? What type of answer are you looking for? Because I can give you the answer you want."

Realizing that I wasn't getting anywhere with this line of questioning, I quickly changed tack: "What would you do with extra money if you could access a cheaper loan?"

"Well, I wouldn't need to go to the market so early every morning to get a loan. I would save a lot of time and I would be able to come here earlier to get a better spot. On days like today, by the time I get here the best places to sell are taken by other women who get to sell more, and are not baking under the sun or getting wet in the rain. I would also save a lot of money in interest. And I could have two baskets of *chipas* every day. I could hire my neighbor's daughter to help me sell more *chipas* on other city corners where there are no sellers." She seemed excited by the possibilities she was describing, and rounded back on my original question. "So how do you want me to answer you? That I'm poor enough to need the loan? Or that I'm doing well enough that I'll be able to repay it? I can give you the answer you want, just as long as you are going to help me and give me a loan."

I wanted her to tell me the truth. Having real data from clients on their economic activities was the only way this was going to work. Microlending is a risky business with only marginal returns. If the Foundation was ever going to achieve financial self-sufficiency we'd need to work at scale, giving lots of loans to lots of clients, using as few staff as possible. Loan Officers would each take on 500–600 clients, organized into 30 or so solidarity lending groups. Having a personal relationship with each and every client was simply out of the question. Instead, we would rely on clients to vet their fellow group members for credit-worthiness and cover anyone who fell short on their twice-monthly repayments. All these things would only work if we believed the clients were being truthful with each other (and with us), rather than just telling us what we wanted to hear.

Yet here was a woman, probably living on or near the poverty line, who was acting non-poor. Or, perhaps more accurately, she was assuming a non-poor identity to blend in against the backdrop of my expectations, like a human chameleon.

Had I been paying attention, I would have heeded the important lesson she was offering me in this real-world classroom. I would have realized I was talking to a woman who refused to be a passive participant in someone else's story about her poverty. I might have seen that poverty is as much about perspective and context as it is about hard data. Instead, I focused on ensuring our internal management systems would cope with client information that might have been unreliable. It's was easy enough oversight to make. When you're setting up a new organization, you want it to run well, and you make a lot of assumptions along the way just to streamline that process. Building blocks first; fine-tuning later.

The following decades were a time of rapid growth for the Foundation. We opened regional offices in the interior of the country, hired staff and developed our internal management and accounting systems. We replaced our typewriters with computers and even bought a fax machine and a photocopier. We were lucky to have Daniel Elicetche, the local Manager of Coopers & Lybrand (later PWC), as our Controller. While he made sure our office ran smoothly, my staff and I were out in the community working with microentrepreneurs to help them grow their businesses. The work was thrilling, exhausting and all-consuming. In fact, it was so all-consuming that I missed my next big lesson on poverty.

The year was 2005, 20 years after my conversation with the woman selling *chipas* on a street corner in the city center. Across town, 15 of our poor microfinance clients gathered in a two-room shack in a riverside slum—and locked the door. They wanted to be in private because they were holding a party. The occasion: their annual pageant and award ceremony. They had all arrived sporting fancy frocks and outrageous makeup. The cramped sitting room became an impromptu catwalk; they took it in turns to parade around to the claps and cheers of the other women. Prize sashes were awarded, after much discussion, to the 'most beautiful' or 'best dressed' of the group. There were prizes for everyone, so no one went home empty-handed. Afterward, they ate cake and toasted themselves with apple cider.

News of the party reached me a few days later—the group's Loan Officer related the story of the event to Luis Fernando, who, in turn, related it to me. When he did, I roared with laughter. "That must be one of the most ridiculous things I have ever heard," I exclaimed. "With all the problems they suffer, they spend money on clothes and makeup instead of on meeting their basic needs? And why did they feel the need to lock themselves in?"

He responded thoughtfully. "Think of it as a question of negative peer pressure. They've been clients for a few years and, while they're still poor, they're better off than some of their neighbors. Some even make more money than their husbands, which doesn't always go down well. They want to celebrate and show off among themselves, but they don't want to be seen doing so. People can be mean, or even violent, when they're jealous—especially in those slums. They don't want others to have what they can't have—to get 'above their station in life'. So it's not just a lack of money that pushes these people down—it's a culture of poverty that *pulls* them down, like crabs in a bucket."

As I watched the students dancing the night away at the 2008 graduation ball at the Cerrito Agricultural High School—chameleons and crabs danced through my mind. And then, finally, I connected the dots. *They were acting like people who weren't poor.*

It seems funny to admit that, until that very moment, I had never examined my assumptions about what it meant to be poor. I couldn't really articulate what it was but – like good art – I knew it when I saw it. *And this is not it*, I thought to myself.

CHAPTER 4
POVERTY

STUDENTS OF THE GLOBAL poverty-reduction agenda will know we weren't the only ones grappling, at the turn of the century, with how to define and measure poverty—and with the question of what we could realistically hope to achieve as a result of our anti-poverty programs. Around that time, the conversation around poverty took two significant turns: the first is that it shifted the unit of analysis from 'nation' to 'individual', and the subject of analysis from 'monetary' to 'non-monetary'.

Briefly: after decades of viewing poverty from the very narrow perspective of money, by 1990 the UN had begun considering a country's overall achievements through the lens of the Human Development Index (HDI), which at the time encompassed five indicators: life expectancy at birth, adult literacy rate, school enrollment rates, mean years of schooling and gross domestic product (GDP) per capita. By 1995, the UN had introduced the Gender Development Index (a gender-lens look at the HDI that highlighted the differences in quality of life outcomes between men and women) and the Gender Empowerment Measure (a composite index of gender empowerment in a country). At once, poverty had gone from black-and-white to technicolor—but we were still measuring it at a national level.

By 2010, the Oxford Human Development Initiative and the UN had introduced a new Multidimensional Poverty Index (MPI), which considered health, education and quality of life through ten indicators: child mortality, nutrition, years of schooling, school attendance, cooking fuel, toilet, drinking water, electricity, flooring materials and physical assets. Importantly, the MPI measured *individual* poverty— enabling policymakers to compare relative poverty levels within countries, between different communities in a country and between different individuals within communities. The theory driving all of this was that the more granular the poverty data, the more effective the anti-poverty programs and policies would be.

In truth, however, I can only tell you all of that because I am viewing it in hindsight. As those debates and breakthroughs unfolded in real time, I wasn't tuned into them at all. Instead, I was focused on what was right in front of me at *Fundación Paraguaya*: how to improve and expand our work on behalf of microentrepreneurs across the country. We opened new branches in new areas, hired new staff and refined our lending methodology where we saw room for improvement. Poverty was the backdrop of that work, of course, and our theory of change was pretty standard fare for the era: if we provide affordable access to small loans, then microentrepreneurs could increase their income and improve their well-being over time.

Implicit in all of this was an understanding of the multi-dimensionality of poverty. How could we not view it in those terms? We were in the houses and communities of our poor clients, day in and day out. We saw the missing teeth, the broken toilets, the underemployed men, the women cooking over open fires, the children running barefoot around the yard instead of attending school. But at the end of the day, microfinance is a fairly blunt instrument of development. Our aim was to help people earn a little more so they could use the additional cash to address those other aspects of poverty we could see in their lives. We hoped that, by solving for income poverty, the other problems would sort themselves out. Social change is a slow, and very complex, process—and we were working on the one issue over which we thought we had a bit of traction.

To even consider the poor as bankable was to swim upstream against the tide of received wisdom in Paraguay (I still wince when I recall that meeting at the National Development Bank). But we were swimming upstream in other ways as well. For instance, we faced considerable pressure to legally transform from a foundation into a commercial bank. 'Best practice' in the microfinance industry in those days held that we could do the most good by growing fast, and to grow fast we'd need a huge injection of private capital. I had reservations about the wisdom of such a move, and I was happy that the Board agreed. Guillermo Peroni, Esteban Burt, Antonio Espinoza, Daniel Elicetche, Amado Adorno, Raul Gauto and a number of other committed professionals and business leaders formed my Board, and actively guarded against anything that might be viewed as mission drift.

The experience of other microfinance foundations transforming into commercial banks, across Latin America and elsewhere, provided us with an important cautionary tale. To deliver market rates of return to their new financial backers, organizations that had once been staunchly pro-poor started moving 'up market', delivering larger (more profitable) loans to less-poor clients, who were a 'better bet' from a risk point of view. *Fundación Paraguaya* wasn't about to forsake its mission on a wild goose chase for glory, for scale and for profit. And why did we need new capital in any event? We had already cracked the nut of financial self-sufficiency, covering all our operational costs using the

money we earned through charging not-unreasonable interest rates to our clients, as well as obtaining commercial loans
from local banks. Transformation would also bring us under
the purview of the national financial regulator, with all the
operational strictures this implied (including jettisoning the
educational component of our work, which we were unwilling to consider).

This was an important concern for us, because enterprise
education was woven into the very fabric of the Foundation.
We knew that simply giving poor entrepreneurs tiny business
loans would be useless if they lacked the skills and knowledge needed to run their businesses well and make the most
of the investment. Successfully delivering the 'education'
component of our 'credit with education' model, however,
had proven a harder task than we had envisioned.

In truth, we underestimated how difficult it would be to
deliver business-management training courses to illiterate
women. In the early days, about a third of our clients could
not read or write. Many could not sign their names. Our Loan
Officers carried inkpads so that our illiterate clients could
print the impression of their right thumb on their promis-
sory notes. That our training didn't work wasn't their fault,
however. It was ours. Or, perhaps more accurately, mine.

I had spent a couple of years teaching business
administration to middle-class students at the Catholic
University of Asunción, and assumed I could simply adapt
this content to the needs of street vendors. I was wrong. The
material we had was difficult to understand. Most of our
clients could not read or write above third-grade level, many
could not even see the blackboard because they didn't have
eyeglasses—and some simply fell asleep during my courses,
exhausted after a long day of work. Rather than seeing any
value in our training courses, clients viewed them as just one
more 'transaction cost' to obtain a cheap loan. By 1987, it
had become painfully clear that our methods and

materials were useless. Clients didn't attend, staff couldn't see the point—and so I made the difficult decision to end the program. It was a disappointment because we understood – or at least we thought we understood – the value of training in improving the lives of clients.

This failure, of course, did nothing to change the fact that the Foundation's bylaws committed us to both entrepreneurial education and income generation support. That we weren't reaching our first objective, and focusing exclusively on financial services, didn't sit easily with the Board. And so it was that, in 1995, when two young local college students, Yan Speranza and Francisco Peroni, approached the Foundation asking for support to develop a youth entrepreneurship program, the Board saw them as a gift from the heavens.

Without hesitation, we offered them office space, salaries and *carte blanche* to implement their Junior Achievement program—on one condition: that they also take their curriculum into the schools our clients' children attended. That way (we rationalized), we'd be delivering both credit and education to our clients in line with our mission—albeit to different members of the same family in the hope that the knowledge would somehow be transferred between generations. (We didn't see it in this way at the time, but it was our first step toward defining poverty at not the individual level but the family level.)

All theory aside: in comparison to our monthly loan-repayment meetings with our adult microfinance clients, those youth-entrepreneurship classes were joyous, raucous affairs. I remember with fondness the thunderous roar of teenage students, raising their hands and clamoring to be noticed, when we stood in front of a classroom and asked: "Who here wants to learn how to make money?"

Knowing I had their complete attention, I'd tell them why we were there: "This twelve-week program is called 'The Company' and you will learn how to run a business and produce something good for society. You'll learn how to make money so that you can be independent from your parents when you are older. First, get together with your best friends in the class and elect your company leaders. Please look at the job descriptions in the booklets you have on your desks. I need you to talk among yourselves and to select five positions: General Manager, Production Manager, Marketing Manager, Human Resource Manager, and Sales Manager. Next week you will have to identify a product that you can make or a service that you can provide. Remember, you must always take the market demand into consideration. It could be a food item that you cook at home; a product, such as printed T-shirts; or a service, such as a car wash. It can be anything, but it has to be something that people are willing to pay money for!"

It's funny, but no matter how many times we launched a new Junior Achievement class, the reaction from students was always the same. It was as if they had never imagined that school could be so fun and engaging. Their excitement was written on their faces as they all talked at once and over each other to share their business ideas, figure out the difference between marketing and sales, and design their business model. They had so much fun that I couldn't help but notice the very stark contrast to the boring business-management evening classes I taught our microfinance clients all those years ago—who, instead of being too excited to sleep, were too bored to stay awake. I was impressed with the Junior Achievement staff; they had found a way to make a dry subject, such as business education, into a captivating subject for the most skeptical of audiences—teenagers.

The Junior Achievement program was not just a success with students—it soon won over teachers, parents and the local press. The Company Program spread to public and private schools; similar youth-entrepreneurship educational programs were soon popping up in the marketplace. A few

47

years later, small companies even began springing up around Asunción as students took their companies to market.

WHILE LUIS FERNANDO AND MY STAFF were busy implementing our microfinance and youth-entrepreneurship programs, I began to take long exploratory trips through the countryside, searching for further opportunities to serve the hard-to-reach young men and women described in our mission statement. It was on one of these trips that I met Brother Aquilino Bravo. A native of Spain, he was short and slim, with a broad smile and the energy of a man on a mission. He was the tenacious Director of the Cerrito Agricultural High School, one of the country's 19 private technical-vocational agricultural high schools for poor young farmers (there were 14 other government schools at the time).

The school didn't charge any significant tuition to families, and it suffered from a lack of funding, government budget cuts and demoralized teachers. To keep his school afloat, Brother Aquilino had even staged protests with teachers and students in front of the Ministry of Agriculture and Livestock and the Ministry of Finance, demanding the government subsidies that had been promised to them.

He was an impressive man doing important work, and I wanted to find ways of supporting him. Brother Aquilino saw a lot of potential in *Fundación Paraguaya's* youth-entrepreneurship program, and we agreed to introduce Junior Achievement programs to his 65-hectare rural campus. We also developed a plan so his students could apply for our microfinance loans upon graduation. Finally, the Foundation also helped the school to develop income-generating alternatives in case the government subsidies fell through.

He was fascinated when he learned how the Foundation could work with the poorest of the poor in urban slums and rural villages, cover its operating costs by charging interest on its loans and run a consistent surplus every year. "I cannot believe the poor can actually pay back their loans with interest," he told me. "I always thought that the poor needed charity hand-outs. There's a lesson in that."

Then, one Friday in October 2002, he phoned me out of the blue. "Martín, we need to talk. I have an urgent matter that I want to discuss with you. Can you come to our campus this afternoon?"

Without hesitating, I cleared my afternoon schedule and headed for my car. I knew that something serious was going on, as I had been talking to him regularly over the past few months. I wasn't prepared, however, for what he would tell me once I arrived.

"Martín," he said, "I just received instructions from my superior that I must go to Rome for an extended period. It's a long spiritual retreat. The only problem is that my fellow brothers are too old to run this school. It is too much work, particularly when government funding is so unpredictable and irregular. I am afraid that we will have to transfer this school to another religious order so that they can try to run it. Unless something happens."

His news felt like such a huge blow. He had worked so hard to keep the school running, even under the constant threat of bankruptcy. I was also puzzled by his last comment. "Something like what?" I asked him.

"Unless someone like you takes over," he responded. "If we could transfer the school to *Fundación Paraguaya*, then you would be able to implement the plans we have been talking about all these past months. If we transfer this school to another religious order, then little will change. The school will continue to depend on government subsidies and life will continue to be miserable for school administrators, teachers and students."

I struggled to grasp the full weight of what he was asking me to do. Sensing my hesitation, he continued. "There is something even more important. I have seen you working. I have been observing you and your team for a few years now. I know that you actually believe that you can help the poor overcome poverty. Not very many people believe that is even possible, Martín. Even among us religious people, many of my colleagues don't believe that poverty can be overcome. They see that poverty is structural, and that overcoming poverty depends on too many outside forces for one person to ever succeed. Many of us in the Catholic Church love the poor. We live among the poor. We even dedicate our lives to educating the poor. But we never for a moment imagine that our students will stop being poor because of our work or our schools. We have seen too many of them graduate and then go back to their lives of misery. They may have learned a thing or two at our technical schools, but they are too small and weak to overcome poverty. You, on the other hand, believe that people can overcome poverty. We respect that very much and we admire your faith in people's capacity to overcome their deprivations.

"More than that, the Foundation already has what it needs to make it succeed. First, you believe that this school can one day become financially self-sufficient, just like *Fundación Paraguaya*. Second, you have a youth-entrepreneurship program that you can combine with the government's technical-vocational curricula. Vocational education alone is not enough, if these students are going to overcome poverty. They need to learn how to grow tomatoes, yes, but they also need to know how to make money growing tomatoes. Your team knows how to teach this. They know how to create special incentives to overcome the aspirations failure that Paraguayan rural youth have.

"Finally, the Foundation has a loan program. What good is it for us to teach students how to grow a crop or raise an animal if they will not have access to a loan to buy the animals and the equipment they need when they graduate?"

I wasn't sure how to respond. In the first place, I had not realized how other people viewed the Foundation. I was also shocked at Brother Aquilino's take on poverty, and surprised by his candor about the Church.

"There is only one problem," he said. "I need your answer in writing by Monday morning."

It was a lot to take in. He was asking us to take over a bankrupt, rural, agricultural boarding school. "Let me consult with my Board of Directors, because this is a big step, and it will cost us a lot of money. But it may be just the right opportunity for us." As I was getting ready to leave, I asked, "Why are you doing this?"

He laughed, responding: "God writes straight with crooked lines."

Driving back to the city, two concerns occupied my thoughts. First, where would we get the money to pay salaries and operating costs? Second, how do I get hold of my Board members on such short notice to have this conversation?

Later that evening at *Fundación Paraguaya's* office in Asunción, five Board members gathered at the conference room for an impromptu meeting. A few were dressed in a suit and tie, having stopped by the office on their way to a formal dinner. Their faces were both grave and amused as they read the draft Memorandum of Understanding I had prepared only minutes earlier. They all knew of my regular visits to Cerrito, and were aware of Brother Aquilino's concerns, but I could see that no one could have anticipated this turn of events. The Memorandum stipulated that *Fundación Paraguaya* would assume ownership of the Cerrito Agricultural High School, cover all its operating costs, make the necessary investment and assure that it would be a boarding school for the poor in perpetuity. All at once, my Board members started asking me all the right questions.

·

"Where are we going to get the money?"

"From the cash reserve we have been accumulating during the past five years in case of an emergency."

"Is it not too risky to leave us without a cash reserve?"

"Yes, it is a calculated risk, but this is an opportunity to serve the people we want to serve."

"Who are you going to put in charge?"

"We have identified an engineer called Jose Luis Salomón, who has the right credentials and is willing to move to the school."

"How long do you think it will take us to reach break-even, so that the school's income will cover its expenses?"

"Probably five years."

"Do you know of another agricultural school that has achieved self-sufficiency?"

"No. I have been researching internationally but have not found anything yet."

"Why do you even think that the school can become self-sufficient?"

"Our microfinance program is self-sufficient and even produces a yearly surplus. It's all a matter of scale. With 50 loans, we could not cover our costs—but by reaching 5,000 clients we cover our operating costs. Why not apply the same logic to the school? With 35 chickens in a demonstration chicken coop, we can never hope to cover costs, but we could with 3,000 chickens because we can sell the eggs and the meat. It is all a matter of scale, good management and cost accounting. We can apply what we've learned in our microfinance program to education."

"Well, I honestly doubt that this will work," admitted Alvaro Caballero, one of my Board members. "However, I vote in favor of this plan. If we are not willing to take risks, then we are not fulfilling our mission." The other Board members agreed.

So it was that, the following week, Luis Fernando and I started drafting an academic-productive business plan. Our challenge was to integrate the Ministry of Agriculture-mandated, technical-vocational, three-year curriculum with our income-generating projects on campus. We quickly learned it would be an uphill battle, especially in terms of the teaching staff we had inherited. For example, the teachers taught students to burn their trash every afternoon, not realizing they were destroying the organic matter needed to maintain the health of the soil. For this reason, we adopted a fully organic agriculture approach to stop the popular custom of raking and burning leaves every day.

In addition, our teachers were accustomed to teaching students how to raise animals and grow crops, but none of what was produced was ever sold outside campus; most of it supplied the school cafeteria, and what was left was given to teachers and staff for free. Teachers and students knew nothing about identifying and satisfying market needs. We needed to add two elements to the traditional 'learning by doing' paradigm: selling farm products and making money.

Finally, we had to tackle the question of *who* our students would be. When we took it over, the boarding school was only for boys, but we wanted to make this opportunity available for young girls as well. We were going to have to recruit female students, designate separate dorms for them, and hire a matron (one Celsa Acosta, who we'll hear more about later) to look after them and guide us on how to change the school's all-boy culture.

In January 2003, we embarked on our ambitious adventure of learning how to run an income-generating, co-educational boarding school. We charged a nominal annual tuition fee; it didn't even cover the cost of meals, but it signaled to parents and students that nothing was free and that school was valuable enough to pay even a little money for. This proved to be the right decision because it allowed us to begin a healthy practice of sharing the school's operational budget with parents and students.

Over time, we also created a range of on-campus educational businesses. Each business was linked to a class and supervised by a teacher. We had an organic vegetable garden, organic crops, chickens, pigs, dairy cattle, rabbits, goats and cheese-making units. Each of these businesses was mandated to cover the costs of running the school and to have a surplus to cover non-income-generating classes, such as math, geography, history, Spanish and so on.

We also transformed a building originally designated for spiritual retreats into a rural hotel, and we added a whole new curriculum to our school: technical-vocational hotel and rural tourism, which proved to be very popular with students. As word spread about the educational quality of the school, we soon expanded it to 150 students—and were running a waiting list.

We left one school business for our final-year students to run by themselves: the school grocery store, which they organized as a Junior Achievement student cooperative. This allowed them to practice their entrepreneurial skills and learn how to make money. Each year, the business was 'sold' – stock and all – to the upcoming senior class.

As the school gained notoriety, we started to receive interesting visitors from other countries—something that surprised us a lot, given the traditional relative isolation of Paraguay. Landlocked in the middle of South America and with few direct flights, our country has always preferred an isolationist attitude toward our bigger and more powerful neighbors, Brazil and Argentina—and to the rest of the world. Suddenly, we were being noticed. Journalists visited and wrote stories about our self-sufficient school. Social leaders from India, South Africa, Nigeria, Nicaragua and elsewhere came to find ways to replicate our model in their countries. Student interns from foreign universities and young professionals came to better understand the 'education that pays for itself' model.

The visibility our educational model created also allowed us to connect with leaders from the corporate and philanthropic world in ways that helped us to advance our own work. One such leader was Duncan Saville, who became a good friend and valuable collaborator (initially by helping us take our educational work to England through Teach a Man to Fish, and also through the School Enterprise Challenge, on which more soon).

Of course, the accolades were gratifying, but for *Fundación Paraguaya* the school represented something far more important. It was the final piece in a virtuous circle that helped us feel, more strongly than ever, that we were really reaching our mission. The Foundation stood for education and income support. We delivered income support to our microfinance clients; entrepreneurial education to clients' children, through our youth entrepreneurship and rural school; and our school graduates then became microfinance clients and successful rural entrepreneurs. It all fit together into one coherent picture, and it felt like the Foundation was making an important contribution to improving the well-being of poor rural Paraguayans.

THAT BEING SAID: if you'd asked us how poor our loan clients were, and whether they were any less poor as a result of our work, I'm not sure we could have given you a clear answer. As was typical of most microfinance organizations of the era, we simply took it for granted that our clients were poor. In fact, our mission statement didn't even include the word 'poverty' back then; it spoke of 'improving the standard of living of microentrepreneurs', but not about 'poor people'.

After all, it's hard to measure something when you don't have a measuring stick.

Still, by targeting our services to urban slums and rural areas, and by offering small loan sizes (which we assumed would be unattractive to better-off people), we were fairly confident in our ability to reach less well-off people in society. What's more, we knew from our tracking data and research that, more often than not, our clients' businesses tended to grow—impact evaluations of our work showed that, after a year in our program, clients tended to create 1.3 new jobs and incomes tended to increase by around 100 percent. These statistics, along with our healthy repayment rate, were enough to convince the Board we were on the right track.

Then again, the signals we were receiving about our clients were mixed. There were clients we worked with for years, and, despite seeing their incomes go up, they still didn't have any teeth. Other clients had stagnant income levels, but when you'd visit them, they'd proudly show off the shiny new modern bathroom they'd just had installed. In short, there seemed to be no consistent relationship between improved income and improved well-being. This was confusing; the 'promise of microfinance' is that, with increasing incomes, well-being improvements will naturally follow. Yet among our clients, each woman had her own unique trajectory, and it was difficult to see how the Foundation influenced any of it.

Take Rosa, for example, a 31-year-old woman living with her husband and three children in Tacupity. She'd been a Foundation client for five years, and was earning $254 a month as a school cleaning lady and by selling cleaning products door to door. Her husband brought home a further $363 every month, which meant this family of five's monthly income was $123 per person—above the national poverty line of $116 per person per month. If we viewed her family's life through the narrow lens of income poverty, we would be forced to conclude they were not poor. Yet her dirt-floor kitchen didn't have four walls, she cooked on an open fire and she didn't own a refrigerator—so can we really think of her as non-poor?

Then there was Eliana, who lived in Santa Rosa del Aguaray. She was married, and supported her family of four by selling clothes and food, bringing home about $545 every month. That put her family's per capita income at $136— well above the poverty line. Yet she didn't have a modern bathroom; her family used a primitive outhouse consisting of little more than four waist-high walls and a hole in the ground. Again: Is this not what poverty looks like?

External evaluations of our work didn't help to clarify the matter in the slightest. One study, conducted by external consultants, used a newly developed metric that compared the country's per capita GNP to our average loan size in order to detect the probability that a person was poor. The report concluded that our clients weren't as poor as we thought they were. Given what we were seeing when we went to our clients' houses, it didn't make sense. After all, what can you really assume about the life of one individual person when comparing the average loan size (of all our clients) against the national average per capita GNP (of everyone in the country)? Can average loan size over average GNP tell you whether the whole family was forced to sleep all together in the same bedroom? Not really. So, in spite of what these 'poverty experts' were telling us, we were certain there was more to the story.

Yet while we had no doubt that poverty was more than a lack of money, we struggled to define precisely what we meant by 'multidimensional poverty' (and, to be honest, we weren't even using that term back then). And so, in January 2008, we invited a consultant to do some exploratory research into the multidimensional poverty of our clients. The results were a real wake-up call for us, but not in the way you might expect.

The evaluator talked to 1,400 clients in two remote rural locations, measuring a range of deprivations. I remember that one of his indicators was 'Potable Water'. After talking to our clients, the consultant concluded that a stunning 96% of our clients had potable water.

Again, having sat in so many of our clients' homes, this result barely seemed possible even to me—but it was one of my Board members, Amado Adorno, who really hit the nail on the head. In our next Board meeting, he was blunt on the matter: "As you know, I own a cattle ranch in that area near Tacuatí, in San Pedro. I've spent a lot of time in that community, and I can tell you for a fact that the indicator is wrong. The consultant asked whether the house had a tap for water. And it's true, most houses do. But having a tap is not the same as having access to potable water, because it doesn't mean you're hooked up to the water service—and even if you are hooked up, most of the time the service is deficient. That's why most of our clients there have water tanks."

THIS IS WHY, standing on the steps of the chapel at our Cerrito Agricultural High School graduation gala in December 2008 with Luis Fernando, our local bishop and Jorge Guerrero, I was having a hard time understanding what I was seeing. The Foundation didn't fully understand what poverty was. We didn't know how to consistently help people overcome poverty. Poverty was a big black box.

Some of our clients increased their incomes; some didn't. Some of our clients grew their businesses; some didn't. Some of our clients dressed up as non-poor people behind locked doors. Some of our clients offered to be non-poor in exchange for a loan, if that was what we preferred. Some of our clients were labeled 'non-poor' by foreigners with clipboards, which didn't line up with what we were seeing.

And now here were these students, suddenly transformed from peasants into aspiring members of the middle class. We were witnessing a mystery, wrapped in an enigma, dressed to the nines and killing it on the dance floor. And it had nothing to do with having increased their income—yet clearly we'd unlocked something inside of them. Identity? Aspiration? What was it?

Whatever it was, it was working. And if it was working for our students, I was sure we could make it work with our microfinance clients, too. I left the graduation ceremony full of hope, full of awe and with the inkling of a good idea.

POOR LUIS FERNANDO. We make a great team, of course, but I think I have the easier time of it. That's because (as our staff likes to tease) it's my job to dream impossible dreams about social change, and it's his job to turn all of those impossible dreams into some sort of operational reality *and* make the books balance.

That is why he was particularly annoyed with me when I called him into my office on the Monday morning after the graduation ceremony.

We agreed that the flair with which our students celebrated their graduation was quite unexpected. I turned to Luis Fernando and said, "Listen, I have been thinking all weekend about what happened last Friday night. I think those kids taught us a big lesson that we need to heed. I felt as though I was seeing our students levitate out of poverty, right before our eyes, right in front of their parents' eyes. Did you get that same feeling? They were almost behaving as if they were middle-class students from middle-class families from middle-class suburbs in the city."

"Yes, the way they wore those elegant clothes and even how they waltzed with their parents. That is something one can see here in the city, but never in the countryside. Our school seems to be a magical place," he responded.

His choice of words took me by surprise. "What do you mean by magical? That school is meant to challenge our students. We recruit young boys and girls from families living in extreme poverty. We even recruit indigenous kids from four different tribes. They get up early in the morning, they sweep and mop the school, they have breakfast, go to classes, then they practice what they learn by working in the different productive units. They follow a rigorous curriculum and schedule, and they only get to go home on weekends when they are not on duty. How is it that such a grinding routine becomes magical and propels our graduating students to have a fairytale gala dinner?" I wasn't so much asking him as I was wondering out loud to myself. "And what about our microfinance clients? Why aren't our clients experiencing this magic? Or are they?"

"Well, our microfinance loan delinquency rate is 2.9 percent. That is magical to me, because it means we have the resources, the people and the surplus for our youth-entrepreneurship program and our agricultural school."

I wasn't interested in his pragmatism in that moment. "Luis Fernando, we must go further, or deeper. I am afraid we may be drifting from our original mission. Last year I saw some pretty big loans going out the door, which could be a signal that we're reaching less-poor clients. Second, many of the poor microfinance clients that we do reach remain poor after years of financial assistance. Some clients grow their businesses, make money, hire people, create jobs, etc. But what about the many clients who are still tiny street vendors ten years later? Why can't our Loan Officers provide their microfinance clients not only loans but also some type of assistance so that they can overcome poverty?"

"We are not in danger of any mission drift. We are right on target. We have three objectives: increase family income, strengthen precarious jobs and create new jobs. That's all we do. We provide loans, and the microenterprises do the rest by themselves. We know that most of our clients are doing well. If we start getting involved in all the other services, our clients will see it as charity, and they won't repay their loans. My advice is that we stick to loans, and our clients will find ways to overcome poverty. Poverty is too complex a matter for us to get involved. Too many issues are intertwined."

"But why be minimalist if we can do better?" I retorted. "Why not address the poverty affecting our clients?"

"Because our model is not broken, so why fix it? Our only objective is financial inclusion, and the more financial services we can provide to our clients, the better for them and the better for us. Our Loan Officers have a clear task: disburse and collect loans. If there is a child without vaccines, or if our clients' children aren't going to school, that is not our problem. There is nothing we can do about that. That is the government's responsibility, not ours."

"The government can't even touch this stuff. They're sitting in some air-conditioned office in the capital. Our Loan Officers are in the clients' homes, they know the harsh reality our clients face. You're telling me that if a Loan Officer visits a client and sees a disabled kid crawling in the dirt because she doesn't have a wheelchair, they will look the other way? Or if there are signs of domestic violence, they won't report it?" I was surprised to hear myself raising my voice, and more surprised to hear Luis Fernando responding in kind.

"No! And I'll tell you why. Because our Loan Officers have clear targets: loan portfolio, number of clients, delinquency rate and profitability. It's just business. A social business, if you will. But we don't do charity."

I ignored this last remark. "We also need a better system to evaluate our work. We have been saying for years that our clients create jobs, and we know roughly how many employees they start with and how many they have a few years later. But is that change because of us? We don't know, because we don't have a control group. Also, we only measure what we do—how many loans we give, how many clients we reach, etc. But we have no idea what's happening in our clients' lives as a result. We need to know what our impact is."

"Well," Luis Fernando responded, coolly, "that is a different matter. If you want to spend our money on hiring an expert evaluator, we can do that. But I don't think that we should mess with our microfinance program. It is a delicate balance that we are managing. Let's not get involved with poverty. It is a quagmire, both for us and our clients. Let's stick to financial inclusion."

"But we must help our clients overcome poverty!" I was shouting again. "We have to make a difference. We cannot just ignore the fact that our clients face unnecessary suffering and that nobody seems to care!"

Luis Fernando stood his ground. "Martín, you aren't making any sense. First you tell me that our loans are too big and that we must reach poorer clients. Then you tell me that we should not only provide them with loans but also help them get wheelchairs. That is crazy. We need to specialize. We can't do everything."

I stared at him in disbelief. We had worked together for too many years to be arguing like this. Finally, I did what I felt I had to do. For the first time ever, I pulled rank on him. "Regardless of what you believe, I am formally instructing you to inform our Regional Managers and our Loan Officers that our new policy here at *Fundación Paraguaya* is to serve poor clients and to develop ways in which they can overcome poverty."

With no small look of defiance, Luis Fernando spoke. "Fine. I will. Just tell me what 'poverty' means, and then I will talk to our Loan Officers."

I was taken aback by the challenge he laid down, and I reached for the first answer I could find: "Well, of course we need to use the Census Bureau's poverty line."

In Paraguay, with the assistance of the World Bank, the government conducted national household surveys and calculated the poverty and extreme poverty lines for urban and rural areas. The poverty line was measured in monetary terms: the minimum amount of money needed to buy food, clothes, shelter and transportation. The extreme poverty line was measured in terms of the money needed to purchase 2,500 calories per person per day, which is another way to say 'no hunger'.

Luis Fernando looked at me squarely. "So. We'll use money to measure poverty? I thought you said that you wanted our Loan Officers to also concern themselves with nutrition and housing or disabilities. Tell me what you want me to tell our Loan Officers. Should they only work with clients living under the poverty line? And then what? Should they help clients create a business plan to generate income above the poverty line? What will our measure of success be? You keep using the word 'poverty'— but what do you really mean when you say it?"

I felt the blood leave my face. After a long, tense silence, I realized my directive had no teeth. I was at a loss, embarrassed and unable to respond.

Luis Fernando was right. If I couldn't articulate what poverty was, I could hardly expect my staff to do anything about it. I had to answer the most important question first. As it turns out, it took me three years to do it.

CHAPTER 5
NOT POVERTY

I WILL ADMIT TO HAVING ASSUMED it would be an easy task to respond to Luis Fernando's challenge, and that I would soon be triumphantly marching into his office with my grand plan. After all, by that point I wasn't wholly unaware of the groundbreaking work being done by Northern academics and policymakers, and I felt certain that the right poverty definition and the right poverty tool were out there somewhere, just waiting for us to adopt; that there were giants ready for me to stand on their sufficiently broad shoulders.

And to a certain extent, I was correct. For someone shopping around for poverty indicators in early 2009, I didn't suffer from a lack of options. What I *did* suffer from was a lack of understanding about what to do with the vast numbers of options in front of me.

At the outset, there were a few things I was certain of. First, I was certain that income wasn't the problem. Or at least, it wasn't the only problem. Our clients faced a wide range of deprivations, and it seemed that having an income wasn't any guarantee they could buy the basic goods and services needed to address them—which is why it wasn't un-common to meet a client doing a brisk trade in her business, but whose child wasn't in school. Likewise, not having an income wasn't any guarantee that a client wouldn't be able to buy basic goods and services—whether that was a smartphone or a new bathroom. The same was true for our students; we hadn't done anything to change their income levels, yet we saw them transform into aspiring members of the middle class. As Luis Fernando rightly pointed out, my task wasn't a matter of benchmarking all our clients against the national income-poverty line and tracking their progress over time. But if it wasn't that—what was it? I needed to find indicators that described all the other forces at play in the lives of our clients. It was then that my deep dive into the literature began.

As early as 1976, the International Labor Organization was talking about poverty in terms of basic human needs, including food, clothing, housing, education and public transportation. On that basis, we'd need to define exact, straightforward, uncontroversial quantitative indicators to describe whether or not a person's human need was met. After all, it couldn't be difficult to measure food, clothing, housing, years of schooling and public transportation. These were all comfortably concrete, observable and (more importantly) measurable according to internationally-comparable standards. A kilo of rice was a kilo of rice everywhere. A food calorie was a food calorie everywhere.

Or was it? I soon learned that 'food' describes a need, not an indicator. What were we meant to be measuring? The quantity of food? The quality of food? The stability of the food supply over the course of the year? Were we meant to look at food in absolute terms (how much food a family could afford) or relative terms (how much food a family could afford compared to their neighbors)? What about the equitable distribution of food within a family? We knew from experience that the women could go hungry within a family that, on paper, had enough to eat. As I explored the literature, these quantitative indicators started to seem anything but uncontroversial and straightforward.

The task in front of me became no less complex once I began to consider not just quantitative but also qualitative indicators. In 1998, Indian economist and Nobel Prize winner Amartya Sen penned his influential *Development as Freedom*. In the book, he offered his 'capabilities approach', which looked beyond the money we need to buy the stuff of life and considered our human dignity, freedoms, human rights, democracy, distribution of wealth, health systems, social protection and culture. By enhancing our human capabilities, Sen argued, we gain more freedom to develop our potential and to do, be and become what we value.

Sen's capabilities approach really resonated with me; it acknowledges that money is only a means to an end and that money isn't the only resource we have. What matters is the freedom people enjoy to live the life they want—and we convert money (and other resources) into the capabilities we need to achieve that freedom. For example, we convert money into food; we convert a bicycle into easy access to market to buy goods. However, there is also a range of personal, social and environmental factors that affect how easy it is to convert a resource (money, bicycle) into a freedom (food, mobility).

For example, a woman may have a bicycle, but the roads to market might be poor, it may be socially unacceptable for women to travel alone or she might be afraid to travel the busy roads to the market. Likewise, if the market is far away, when you factor in the time she might need to spend away from her business to go to market, her goods and services end up costing her more resources than they would cost someone who lived closer to market.

When we account for different conversion factors, we start seeing how the use of a given resource leads to a different well-being outcome for each individual. Hence, people may be 'poor' even if they have money, or they may be 'not poor' even if they don't have money.

While this capability approach had many notable followers, the work of one woman in particular proved a valuable guide through its new poverty landscape: Sabina Alkire, Co-Founder of the Oxford Poverty and Human Development Initiative (OPHI) (coincidentally, she co-founded OPHI with John Hammock, a former Executive Director of Accion, the organization that helped us start our microfinance program). Around the time we first met (at a conference in Prague, where she gave me one of her excellent articles), she was focused on grounding the capability approach within the Multidimensional Poverty Index (MPI), a weighted index that encompasses years of schooling, school attendance, child mortality, nutrition, electricity, sanitation, drinking water, flooring materials, cooking fuel and asset ownership. All these aspects of poverty influence whether a person can achieve their potential; they are also comfortably measurable.

The MPI is a weighted index that encompasses years of schooling, school attendance, child mortality, nutrition, electricity, sanitation, drinking water, flooring materials, cooking fuel, and asset ownership. All of these aspects of poverty influenced whether a person could achieve their potential, while at the same time being comfortably measurable.

But did that solve our problem and provide us with the poverty metric we needed? Not quite, because each choice of indicator carried built-in assumptions about how to measure it, which in turn had knock-on effects in terms of the cost, ease, quality and reliability of the data-collection process, as well as how useful the data would be for making different types of decisions. For instance, were we collecting poverty data to make general statistical inferences about the population (in which case a sample-based survey would be fine), or did we want qualitative insights we couldn't necessarily generalize (in which case we'd need to do focus groups)? Did we want to use other people's data (such as from the national census) or collect our own? Did we want the data-collection process to be empowering (like a participatory exercise) or extractive (structured interviews); quick (a short survey with all clients) or more in-depth (a lengthy interview with only some clients)? How would we track and understand how these indicators changed over time? How would we understand how much of that change was due to the work of the Foundation? Did we want our data to tell us what was happening in the lives of our clients, or what was happening *and why*? Would we measure actual satisfaction of needs (e.g. being healthy) or the potential satisfaction of needs (e.g. living near a health clinic)? Who was going to use all this data, how often did they want to use it and how did this impact our choice of indicators (because there's no point in trying to make daily decisions based on data you only collect once a year)?

Is your head spinning yet? Mine definitely was. The more I learned about poverty methodologies, the more I learned just how little I really knew. I was sure that the multidimensional definition of poverty was the right choice for us—but that led me down a road that had too many options to consider, too many decisions to make without knowing how to make them. I was overwhelmed.

Luckily, I was part of networks (such as the Avina Foundation, Synergos, Skoll Foundation, Eisenhower Fellowship and the Schwab Foundation for Social Entrepreneurship) that put me in touch with colleagues doing similarly innovative work, who were generous with their time and advice. One such person was educator Taddy Blecher, who was introducing transcendental meditation into his work with underprivileged youth in Johannesburg. Another was Vera Cordeiro, a medical doctor who had started visiting her patients' homes in the *favelas* of Rio de Janeiro after realizing no amount of hospital care would suffice if their living conditions (including clean water and good nutrition) were unhealthy. In those moments, when I grappled with the limits of my own knowledge and skills, it was fellow change-makers from around the world who shared the insights and encouragement I needed to keep going.

It was time to pause and go back to first principles. It struck me that focusing on *how we wanted to use* our poverty tool might just be an effective sorting mechanism for all the design choices I needed to make about what data to collect, how to collect it, when to collect it and who would collect it.

It also occurred to me that reverse engineering our tool, based on how we wanted to use it, would lead us to create a methodology that looked vastly different to everything else available at the time. That's because all the poverty frameworks, approaches, tools, indices and indicators I had studied focused on just one thing: measurement. They all measured in different ways with different units of analysis and produced different results, but at the end of the day, all you were left with was a label: *very poor, poor, not poor.*

In contrast, I wanted our tool to be something we could use to both diagnose and alleviate the problem. As my colleague Andy Carrizosa put it: if poverty were a headache, we wanted to invent a thermometer made out of aspirin. With this end goal in mind, things suddenly started getting clearer. Because I wanted our tool to serve this dual purpose, I assumed we didn't want to measure any aspect of poverty (such as freedom of speech) that we had no hope of influencing directly. Therefore, we would limit our list of indicators to those that were directly actionable. I also knew I wanted this tool to be easy to understand – and easy to use – by both the staff members applying the tool and the clients to whom they were applying it. I wanted it to give us a comprehensive picture of a person's poverty, but not be so unwieldy we couldn't manage it. We wanted to apply this tool ourselves, so external researchers were out. We wanted to collect our own data;

external data was out. We wanted a tool that was flexible and powerful but cost-effective to apply and manage. But first, we needed to identify the right indicators.

With this vision firmly in mind, I returned to my literature review and pulled out what I thought were the most likely candidates for indicators we could use. Within the space of a few months, I had studied every poverty-measurement tool, approach or theory available at the time, including OPHI's MPI, the World Bank's Poverty Line, the International Labor Organization's Basic Human Needs approach, Amartya Sen's Capabilities Approach, the International Fund for Agricultural Development's Sustainable Livelihoods Approach, the United Nations' HDI, the Millennium Development Goals and the Paraguayan National Planning Agency approach, as well as work coming out of the Chronic Poverty Research Centre at the University of Manchester, the World Health Organization, Canada's International Development Research Centre and the International Council of Voluntary Agencies, and the poverty-measurement tools promoted by the Microcredit Summit Campaign (which were the Grameen Bank's Progress out of Poverty Index, the USAID Poverty Assessment Tool, the CASHPOR Housing Index, the Participatory Wealth Ranking approach, the FINCA Client Assessment Tool and the Consultative Group to Assist the Poor Poverty Assessment Tool).

By that point, I was living, breathing and dreaming multidimensional poverty indicators. I was convinced that I was now in possession of each and every potential poverty indicator (and an absolute bore at dinner parties). As far as I could discern, no other tool available was used for both poverty diagnosis and alleviation. But that didn't mean I couldn't draw on similar indicators; it just meant I would use them in a different way. And I was starting to feel confident that I'd be able to do just that. The only thing left was to figure out which, from that huge pile of indicators, would be most relevant to our clients. There was only one place I could go to find out the answer.

FEBRUARY 2009. It was lunch time and I was in Villarrica, a small town of 26,000 inhabitants in the interior of Paraguay, a three-hour drive to the east of Asunción. *Fundación Paraguaya's* office there was small, too, consisting only of one Secretary, one Cashier, three Loan Officers and an Office Manager. The team managed a rapidly growing portfolio of 5,000 clients. That day, the Office Manager assembled his staff and a dozen or so microfinance clients, who happened to have stopped by to make a loan repayment that day. We sat in a big circle in the courtyard under a shady mango tree. One member of our staff distributed *tereré* (a typical Paraguayan tea) to everyone gathered. It was my fifth such meeting that month, and I was eager for the introductions to be over so we could begin.

When it was my turn to speak, I started by describing the journey I had been on. "I am visiting all of our offices in different parts of the country so that I can speak to clients and staff, just like we're sitting down today. Why am I on this journey? Because I would really like to hear your thoughts on one very important question. That question is: in our country, what does it mean to be 'not poor'?"

The discussion that followed was similar to all my previous discussions. The talk was animated and forthright. Never once did I experience an awkward silence. Both clients and staff were eager to talk about poverty (some of our staff had themselves grown up in poor households). The only way I can describe it is to say it was almost as if they had been *waiting* for someone to ask them that very question.

I recorded important insights in my notebook, struggling to keep up with the pace of the conversation.

"To be not poor, it's important to have money," one woman offered.

"Yes, you need enough money to cover your family's needs. If you have children, you should buy clothes and school supplies," another woman added.

"Government services are also important, especially in health. Our problem here is that the public health post is far away," said a Loan Officer.

"Education is important," noted a client, "but it's more important to know your way around. I have a neighbor who went up to sixth grade, but she is not as hardworking and capable as me, and I only went up to third grade. But I also realize that my children should not suffer as much as me, so I spank them whenever they want to miss school. I will make sure they graduate from high school."

The *tereré* and the conversation kept flowing. Talking with clients and staff about what it meant to be 'not poor' was the easy part. The difficult part would be to distill those conversations into a coherent and comprehensive list of indicators that was long enough—but not too long. What's more, we wanted to define three thresholds within each indicator: what it meant to be 'not poor' in that indicator, what it meant to be 'poor' and what it meant to be 'very poor'.

To try to tease out these distinctions, I chose what I hoped would be a relatively straightforward indicator. "Can you tell me more about water? How much water do you need to be considered *not poor*? We know that everybody drinks at least some water or else they would be dead—so we cannot say that being not poor means you drink water, and you're poor if you don't. So what is the difference between *poor* and *not poor*? Is it about the type of water you drink?"

"It all depends," a client said. "In this part of the country, if you have a faucet of treated water in your house, or even in your yard, you are not poor in water. You have less risk of getting sick. Nobody can say that you are poor in water if you have a faucet. If you have a faucet, it usually means that your water comes from the government water company or from a local water board. Usually, that water is treated for human consumption. If you have a well, you are poor but you are also not very poor. You are in the middle."

"You are telling me that if a person has only one faucet, even if it's outside in the yard, she is not poor?" I asked, recalling how one of my Board members said that the faucet indicator proposed by an external expert was not useful, because most people have a faucet but many are not connected to a constant and clean water supply. "So, what is being poor in water?"

"Well, it could be many things," another client interjected. "For example, you are poor in water if, even if you have access to drinking water, that water is not constant and sometimes you don't have water most of the day. It could also be that you only have a well and you don't have a water tap, a faucet. Or it can be that there is a faucet of treated water, but it is a block away from your house. There are many ways in which you can be poor in water," she said.

"What about being very poor in water? Is there a difference?" I asked.

Here, a Loan Officer chimed in. "Yes, a huge difference! I have seen some of our clients who drink water that is not safe for humans. They get their water from a reservoir or a stream where animals drink. Many people get sick from the water they drink. I've seen others whose source of water is far away from their homes, even a kilometer or so, and they must bring water in buckets on their head. To me, that means they're very poor."

"Tell me about housing? What is a good house? What is a poor house?" I asked.

"Oh, a house must be safe," said a client. "It must have at least a roof, windows, and doors."

"It must have separate bedrooms so that adults have intimacy," said another.

"Not only for the adults' sake. Sometime stepfathers want to get fresh with their stepdaughters," said another. Instead of pursuing that line of thought, I nodded and wrote 'domestic violence' on my notepad.

"It must have a ventilated kitchen so we are not breathing smoke all the time."

"It must have elevated stoves so children don't get burned with the charcoal, or to prevent the animals in the house from eating our food."

"It must have a sanitary latrine."

"It must have a refrigerator, or at least someplace to keep food fresh."

"It must have tables and chairs, so people are not eating on their beds."

"A home must have a minimum set of utensils."

"What else?" I asked. "What about transportation?"

"Yes, that's important," a lady said. "But I think that faith in God is the most important thing. At least in my case, the Virgin Mary keeps me going."

"Yes, faith is important," added another client. "But I think that the family is the most important thing. If you have a strong family, if parents provide a good upbringing, if there is someone that children can go to for advice, then that child will most likely not be poor. That is true in my case, at least."

I loved these interviews. Some were short and sweet, some were long and involved and some were full of contradictions. Regardless, they helped me keep my feet on the ground. To help me process this treasure trove of insights, I started to pull other members of the Foundation into my work. I delighted in bringing them a fresh set of interview notes, which we used to complete and refine our evolving set of indicators and thresholds. If you'd stopped by when we were having one of those early discussions, you might have assumed we were making good progress in answering The Big Question:

'What is poverty?' You would have learned that while we, too, grappled with contradictions, we always found a clear consensus, at the end, of what it meant to be 'poor', 'non-poor' and 'very poor' for each indicator. Yet one problem nagged at me.

I was interested to learn that poor people intuitively knew that drinking clean, treated water was important and that vaccinating kids was important. Yet they felt that having a positive attitude and family influence were also key determinants of whether a person would be poor or not. And, if I'm honest, this is where I started feeling I was getting in over my head. Multidimensional poverty, to my mind at least, meant we'd measure things that weren't about income but were still observable and objectively measurable. You can use a faucet. You can inspect a roof. You can confirm whether the kids are in school. You can visit a latrine.

But how were we meant to measure something as vague as 'positive attitude' or 'faith in God'? Should we even be trying to measure things we can't observe, and if so, how? How many kilos does confidence weigh? What is the ground speed of joy? What is the street value of cultural traditions? Our clients were telling us what is meant to be 'not poor' but were naming things that were internal, subjective.

Returning to the poverty literature did nothing to help me understand the question of subjectivity. If anything, it only heightened my bewilderment. By all accounts, the problem with subjective indicators is the issue of precisely where that subjectivity lies—and it gets to the very heart of our understanding of the nature of reality. One key question dominated this discussion: to what degree was reality an independent entity from the person experiencing that reality? Is poverty an objective reality we can objectively measure? Or is it an objective reality whose measurement depends on how we subjectively perceive it? And, even if that poverty could be objectively measured, does the very act of measuring it introduce a subjective layer of interpretation on top of it? In other words, does the reality of a person's poverty change depending on who is measuring it and how they perceive that poverty? Or is poverty an entirely subjective experience that is created by the measurement of it? The mere fact that I was asking these kinds of questions made me feel as though I was getting in over my head—never mind whether or not I'd be able to answer them.

Even assuming I would be able to get to grips with subjective indicators, I wasn't sure whether it was possible to integrate both subjective and objective indicators into one tool. Maybe it was possible, but was it desirable? If no one had done it before, was it because they knew more about field research than I did? That was more or less the point when my head started spinning, and when my triumphant march into Luis Fernando's office started looking more and more like a case of wishful thinking.

During our next Board meeting, I confessed my fears to my colleagues. On the one hand, it felt like we were on to something; my conversations with clients had not only affirmed what the literature was telling me but also opened up a whole new landscape of possibilities in terms of how to define poverty. Yet if I couldn't figure out how to integrate objective and subjective indicators into one tool, all that work would have been for nothing.

"Have you heard of a psychologist named Ken Wilber?" came the reply from Jorge Talavera, a Board member. "You should learn more about what he calls *integral theory*."

Honestly, I was so desperate that I ran to the bookstore as soon as the meeting ended.

CHAPTER 6
SUBJECTIVITY

A CRISP MAY MORNING in Denver, Colorado, is a special kind of pleasure. It was 2010 and I was loitering in Ken Wilber's living room, gazing out over the snow-topped Rocky Mountains, waiting for him to appear. I was grateful that he'd accepted my request for an interview, and equally surprised to find that I was just one of a roomful of people waiting to interview him. (To the extent that Wilber was the leader of a new, global, transcendental philosophical movement, it might be more accurate to say I was in a room full of people *waiting for an audience with him*. But that's beside the point.)

I hadn't come unprepared. In the months leading up to our interview, I had read (and re-read) his books, *A Brief History of Everything* and *Integral Psychology*. As someone struggling to understand how to fit two seemingly different ways of under-standing poverty into one methodology, I found his writing to be both challenging and reassuring. For those unfamiliar with his work, it's worth reviewing the broad outlines.

Since time immemorial, humankind has witnessed thinker after thinker step up to the podium to try to explain *why things are the way they are* and *how they got to be that way*. I don't doubt that you're familiar with many, if not most, of these thinkers, worldviews and fields of study: rationalism, Confucianism, empiricism, humanism, atheism, communism, national socialism, capitalism. Ecology, geology, meteorology, biology, chemistry, botany. Systems theory, chaos theory, complexity theory. Legal positivism. Newtonian physics. Quantum mechanics. The Big Bang theory. Creationism. Creative destruction. Macroeconomic theory. Plato. Heidegger. Locke. Malthus. Samuel P. Huntington. Jared Diamond. Here, too, we could include any one of the poverty theories I'd been studying—those who perceive poverty to be a structural problem or a character flaw, or a failure of government, of the market, of society.

And while these theories and worldviews all might have a degree of internal coherence and appear to explain a great many things, they all fail to do one simple thing: *explain everything.* (Wilber would also point out, I think with a wry smile, that even the so-called 'theory of everything' emerging from the world of physics can't explain why I don't like opera all that much.)

Is this a problem? Not necessarily—until we use those theories to justify the way we choose to organize our societies and governments, and until we consider that, among this surfeit of not-entirely-satisfactory worldviews, we have competing worldviews that suggest different ways of organizing our societies and governments. So which is the more correct: Capitalism or communism? Big government or small government? Christianity or Islam? Right to life or right to choose? Setting aside the fact that debates, elections and even wars are fought over questions such as these, the only thing we can be certain of is that, for all our theories, we're no closer to knowing the truth, knowing the right answer. Nothing is certain; everything is relative. Pluralism has robbed us of the comfort of there being one single truth—and without truth, there can be no progress. Thus, the great engine of human consciousness seems to have stalled. We live in a pluralistic society, and when everything is relative, nothing can ever be true.

Enter Wilber. His aim is to move us from the plural to the integral. Integral theory starts with the recognition that every human theory (spiritual, economic, political, social, psychological or otherwise) contains an element of truth, that they are all part of a larger integral truth and that they can be mapped onto one simple quadrant. This quadrant divides the world in a number of ways. The first division is into individual and collective realms; the second is into subjective and objective realms (see Figure 1).

Along these lines, the subjective world consists of individual thoughts and beliefs, as well as collective cultures and values. None of these can be directly observed; instead, they must be arrived at through dialogue. The objective world can be empirically measured at the individual level (as seen in what we do and what we own) and the collective level (as seen in how we organize our society and our institutions).

While subjective states aren't subject to empirical measurement, they can often be detected through objective means. For example, I can describe my fears to you (individual subjective) or you can track my brainwave patterns in response to a stimulus (individual objective). The collective stories that make up our shared culture (collective subjective) can be detected, thanks to the advance of movable type printing, and shared via internet communications technology (collective objective).

That being said, Wilber's view is that while all human theories can be mapped onto these quadrants, rarely do they span two or more realms. In fact, with very few exceptions, they tend to completely ignore the existence of the other realms within the map. Hard science ignores spiritual faith; empiricism rejects the validity of folk wisdom.

Figure 1: An integral view of the world

	SUBJECTIVE	**OBJECTIVE**
INDIVIDUAL	**Includes:** Thoughts, beliefs, emotions, attitudes, intentions **Described by:** Freud, Jung, Piaget, Buddha	**Includes:** Behavior, speech, assets, health, wealth **Described by:** Skinner, Watson, Locke, physics, biology, neurology
	THOUGHTS	**BEHAVIOR**
	CULTURE	**SYSTEMS**
COLLECTIVE	**Includes:** Shared values, folk wisdom, cultural norms, dominant worldviews, semantics **Described by:** Kuhn, Weber, ethics, sociology, anthropology, mythology	**Includes:** Social systems, ethnic tribes, IT networks, political parties, financial markets, ecological systems **Described by:** Systems theory, Marx, Smith, complexity theory, chaos theory

Why is any of this relevant to the question of poverty? Well, let's consider the case of a poor person who is suffering from a communicable disease (a not-unthinkable scenario). It's not just the hard scientific (individual objective) view of the person's state of health that matters. That person's ability to cope with the disease (individual subjective) is also influenced by whether there's a cultural stigma attached to having that disease (collective subjective) and whether the country has sufficient health infrastructure (collective objective).

Even conventional poverty theories can be mapped onto this quadrant. In fact, it wasn't until I did so that I was able to rationalize why they were so divergent and how they all fit together into one coherent whole. The *individual objective* view of poverty focuses on lack of income and assets. The *individual subjective* view of poverty views it as the product of a personal defect (you're dull-witted and lazy). The *collective subjective* view of poverty is described by the Calvinist virtues (wealth is God's reward for your hard work). The *collective objective* view is that poverty is structural—it's due to inadequate health services, transportation and schools, among other things.

On a gut level, Wilber's philosophy made sense to me; at least, it helped me to view the seemingly competing poverty worldviews as part of a bigger picture—as interlocking ways of looking at the same problem. Then again, I had no idea how knowing this would help me to design an anti-poverty methodology. I hoped to find some answers in Colorado.

AS WE MET, I was immediately struck by the calm that Ken radiated. He towered over me, yet barely seemed to take up any space in the room. In contrast to my typically animated demeanor, he had a singular focus that seemed to make the rest of the world melt away. It was an intense conversation, in more ways than one.

I explained my work to develop an anti-poverty methodology, and that I was running into a wall that could only be explained by quoting Tolstoy's unappealing dictum: 'Happy families are all alike; every unhappy family is unhappy in its own way.' How could I hope to bring every type of unhappiness (or deprivation) into one methodology?

"Tolstoy is a good place to start, actually," Ken began. "While everyone might be unhappy – or poor – in their own way, it's important to see them holistically. You can only understand poor people if you understand their exterior world – their individual behavior and the social system they live in – and their interior world, by which I mean their individual beliefs and intentions, and their collective culture."

"I guess so, but the problem is that each quadrant represents a completely different way of looking at poverty indicators. How can I have one methodology that includes objective things like clean water as well as subjective religious beliefs? I can name seven different economists that will tell me I'm crazy."

"My friend, welcome to the world of integral. Both the subjective and the objective realms are telling their own truths, and they're both correct. In this country, for example, the political Right focuses on interior factors such as values, work ethic, dignity and motivation. The political Left tends to focus on exterior factors such as economic disparity, social exclusion, environmental degradation and technological systems. There is an external world where physical things can and must be measured objectively and empirically. There is also an internal world that must be measured subjectively, hermeneutically. Neither one is invalid."

"Hermeneutically?"

"It means that some things you just can't measure empirically. For example, 'self-esteem' is a social construct. It is what people in a village, a university or a society agree that it is through dialogue. There is no such thing as a universally correct answer, and our answers can change over time. A person with high self-esteem can be described as an egotistical, selfish person in one culture, and as a loving person with empathy toward others in another culture. What it is depends on the meaning that is assigned to the phrase 'self-esteem' by those discussing it. It is a subjective interpretation, whereas a ton of bricks is always a ton of bricks."

"So, you're saying it is acceptable to use both objective and subjective indicators to understand poverty?"

"Not only is it acceptable, but it is also essential if you are going to understand the whole spectrum of human existence. Don't worry about sticking with just one approach. Different development maps have been created by different authors, all of them authorities in their fields. They all contain different perspectives of the same truth—and you can embrace different theories and come up with a coherent methodology that honors different fields. There is a place for anthropology to understand how women behave in one of your microfinance groups, and there is a place for the carrot and stick approach in psychology. Your preference for microfinance does not mean that you cannot understand people's faith or trust in a higher being to assist them in their time of need. Or that people's needs for drinking water or vaccines are incompatible with people's need for love or aesthetic appreciation. When a child breastfeeds, does the nurturing come only from the mother's nutritious milk or from the holding, the embracing, the sense of love and security that the mother provides?"

"I hear what you're saying, but I can't see how I can integrate drinking water and love into one single measure."

"What you call 'multidimensional poverty' reminds me of Howard Gardner's multiple intelligences. Gardner says that development involves not one capacity but many relatively independent capacities. He says that each person has different capacities, be it musical, mathematical, artistic or athletic. Each of those capacities develops in its own way, in its own time and according to its own logic. And remember: just because someone is great at the piano doesn't mean they're great at everything. They might be terrible at doing sums, or remembering to send birthday cards."

"So, what you are telling me is that one can be 'talented' in self-esteem and less 'talented' in money? That would mean we'd need to consider all of these indicators individually, rather than combining them into one poverty index, like all the other approaches."

"Of course. Didn't you tell me that all unhappy families are unhappy in their own way? How can a weighted index – one number or score – possibly communicate the richness of their experience as a poor family?"

"That would mean we'd need to create a whole map for each family. It would be impossible to manage!"

"Perhaps not."

"Well, even if it weren't, I still don't see how we get at the interior dimensions."

"No one can see what another person feels and intends to do. Only that person knows, so only that person can tell you."

He nodded and stayed silent as I tried to work out the implications of everything I was hearing. "So I could design some sort of questionnaire with lots of different poverty indicators. And...I could organize them by dimension, I guess? I should group them in four categories such as intentions, behavior, culture and systems?"

"No," he responded, "it's not about dividing your indicators by whether they are individual or collective, objective or subjective. You must see all of these dimensions within each indicator. The indicator describes the deprivation. It tells you what is wrong. The dimensions help you to understand *why* that person is poor in that indicator. Each of the indicators that you are compiling, be it water or income or self-esteem, will have four faces, four dimensions. And if you want to use this methodology to eliminate the deprivation, you need to know why it's happening. Think about it."

An integral approach to poverty measurement was starting to come into focus. I closed my eyes and tried again. "So, in practical terms what you are telling me is that we must learn to see the poor people with whom we are working from four perspectives: individual, collective, interior and exterior. For example, when we are confronted with, say, a poor client with no front teeth—the Loan Officer must be trained to ask the reasons behind this deprivation from four points of view. First, whether it is because she does not take care of her teeth or has bad nutrition, which entails behavior. Second, whether it is because there is no dentist nearby, which is related to a lack of health infrastructure. Third, whether it is because in her culture, for a person older than 65 years old, it is culturally acceptable to not have front teeth if the person is poor. And fourth, whether she does not have teeth because she is afraid of going to the dentist; that is, whether she has no intention of accessing health care even if it were available. And we need to know which one it is so we know how to support her. Right?"

"See? Once you get started, it's not that difficult."

"Let's take low income, for example. Our Loan Officer will ask the following questions: Why doesn't she have any money? Is it because she does not sell more than two dozen *chipas* a day, which is related to behavior? Is it because there are no microfinance services in her urban slum—the system? Is it that in her village it is not considered appropriate for an older lady to sell food door to door—her culture? Or is it that she does not want to sell more *chipas* because she would rather take care of her grandchildren—her intention?"

"Yes. For your poverty methodology to work, you have to consider all the quadrants for your indicators and recognize that, as Tolstoy might say, two people can be poor in the same indicator for completely different reasons. And knowing the reason behind the problem you've identified is the essential precondition for using your methodology to solve it."

I could have stayed with Wilber all day, but I was keenly aware of the other people waiting to speak with him. I was grateful for this visit, and I did not want to overstay my welcome.

"Before you leave," he offered, "There is another thing to remember, and that's the question of perspective. We're all climbing up the ladder of consciousness—and each person, rich or poor, has a personal perspective, and we always mistake perspective for truth. Yet each person's perspective is unique according to which wall their ladder is leaning against, and depending on which rung of the ladder they are standing on. We can understand the rungs below us that we've already climbed, but not the ones above us that we have yet to climb. Think of it this way: An atom cannot understand the molecule, but the molecule can understand the atom. The molecule can't understand the cell, but the cell can understand the molecule. Likewise, a person who sees the world from their lower rung in the ladder cannot see what a person on a higher rung can."

"Does that mean we all see the world in our own way, according to where we are on the ladder of development? So, as a middle-class person, when I see a poor person throwing their trash out of a bus window, I would think they are dirty because they are littering, which is bad for the environment. But from their perspective, they are cleaning their seat on the bus, and that's a good thing. Or the person who sweeps their yard and leaves their trash on the street sees themselves as a clean person?"

"Exactly. They are being rational in their own way. They are operating from a lower level of consciousness. They will never be able to see other people's perspective unless they can put themselves on that rung of the ladder leaning against the same wall."

"That's interesting, but what does that have to do with the poverty methodology?

"It means that people have to be assisted to climb their ladder of their awareness. You can't just plug your knowledge into their head, because it won't work in the way you expect it will."

"Yes, that sounds familiar. It's what Paulo Freire suggested in his book *The Pedagogy of the Oppressed*, which the Jesuit priests at my high school often quoted from. He proposes that students should not be considered empty vessels to be filled with knowledge, but people who need to be made aware of their own lack of knowledge. He coined the term *concientización*, which is like saying 'understanding' or 'awareness'. Funnily enough, most development organizations do 'plug' new information into the heads of their beneficiaries. We call it 'capacity building'. But as you say, it doesn't always lead to improved results."

"Precisely. Now: one final word of caution. Who does the measuring of poverty, Martín? And who owns the poverty? If we were thinking about medicine, who owns health—the doctor or the patient? You mentioned that if you believed that every poor family is poor in their own way, then it would be impossible for you to manage the poverty methodology. So, I repeat, whose poverty is it? Is it yours and the other good people who are working with you? You also have your own perspective and your own way of seeing things because of the specific characteristics of your ladder and your wall. When you draw a map of poverty, you must take into consideration the map-maker, yourself. The map-maker, no matter how hard he tries, cannot be left out. That even applies to me, drawing the map of integral theory. What makes sense to me might not make sense to everyone. Therefore, you must remember that the poor have their own perspective. If they are encouraged to identify the deprivations they suffer, they are being asked to map their poverty. They themselves must be included in their poverty map."

"Thank you for your time, Ken," I said, and offered my hand to shake his. Instead, he embraced me.

"Today you taught me a great lesson. If the key to understanding poverty is to overcome duality and to find oneness, then by definition we are all part poverty and part non-poverty. You will see that, as you search for answers, you will find that many of the poverty indicators apply to you and me. We are all poor, Martín."

As I left, I'm not sure I fully appreciated the implications of this last reflection. Nevertheless, my head buzzed with new ideas and new possibilities—of a poverty map that explored the unique landscape of a person's poverty; of awakening a person's awareness to the reasons for their deprivations in a way that helped them to act. But I had no clue how I was meant to create this map, whose map it was or how to help people move from awareness to action.

As it turns out, I found part of the answer in those same mountains, but to the west—in Utah.

CHAPTER 7
INFLUENCING

FOR ALL OF OUR carefully laid plans, sometimes it's easy to overlook the role that serendipity plays in life. And, as it turned out, serendipity was waiting for me when I stepped out of my rental car in Sundance Village, Utah, shortly after my conversation with Ken Wilber. Sundance is a beautiful valley flanked by impressive mountains. In those mountains, I would spend a few days walking and talking with individuals who would change the face of my work forever.

Ostensibly, I was in Sundance, at the invitation of the Skoll Foundation, to meet with film producers and directors who wanted to document the work of *Fundación Paraguaya's* financially self-sufficient agriculture schools. But I also took advantage of the opportunity to meet an old friend and colleague, Dave Peery. Dave's family foundation was (and still is) an active supporter of, and vocal advocate for, the work of *Fundación Paraguaya*. More importantly, though, I had come to cherish Dave as a thought partner; a fellow radical and dreamer who is never complacent about the global fight to eliminate poverty. On one of our many walks, we quite literally bumped into one of Dave's old college professors, Todd Manwaring, who was also there to take in the sun, air and scenery—and who was, by luck, accompanied by one of his best friends, Joseph Grenny.

Joseph Grenny is widely known as 'the behavioral science guy'. He is a business strategist and author; his book *Influencer: The New Science of Leading Change* is one of his many *New York Times* bestsellers. His insights and expertise meant he held an important key that would unlock my understanding of how to eliminate poverty. As we sat at a picnic table in the sun, I related to him the story of my work, the challenges I was facing and how Ken Wilber had turned so many of my ideas about poverty on their head. I told him I wanted to create a methodology that would describe the range and severity of a family's unique deprivations, correctly identify the reasons for those deprivations and use that information to permanently eliminate them.

"That's a compelling vision," Joseph offered. "But at the end of the day, you're not the one that can eliminate the poverty. You're just the influencer."

"Yes, I think that our work is built around that assumption. Microfinance is all about self-help; clients do 99 percent of the work. Our youth-entrepreneurship programs all use project-based learning. Our agricultural schools are places where students learn by doing—not just how to farm, but how to make money farming. But this is what I'm struggling with: Microfinance is about just one thing—increasing income. The agricultural school is about just one thing— running a profitable farm. In both cases, the narrow focus makes them feel manageable. But now I'm faced with a long list of poverty indicators which all need to be measured and tackled individually, and maybe in different ways once we start looking at the four different dimensions of each indicator. It all feels a little overwhelming."

"Yes, I can see that. And while Wilber may have described four different dimensions – behavior, systems, culture and intentions – my best piece of advice is that you focus only on behaviors."

"That sounds right. All of our indicators have to be about things that people can control, which I guess is another way of saying 'behaviors'. For example, there's no use in having one of our indicators be the national infant mortality rate, because what can a poor person, or a Loan Officer for that matter, do about a national statistic? But we can have an indicator about good breastfeeding or vaccination behavior, for example. Is that what you're talking about?"

"Partly, yes. But it's more than just actionable indicators. What are the actionable solutions to improve the result of any given indicator? Focus on a few behaviors, the right behaviors, that influence whether a person achieves a given indicator or not. Your job now is to find out what those key behaviors are—but the good news is that you don't have to look far. All you need to do is look for instances where a poor person is doing really well in an indicator despite the odds. For example, in a family that has great nutrition despite having a low income—find out what they're doing differently than everyone else who has *both* low income and poor nutrition."

"Or a poor single mother who manages to send all of her kids to high school?"

"Precisely. We call these stories *positive deviants*. You can also identify *make-or-break moments* in a process—when, for any given indicator, things are most at risk of going wrong. For example, factory workers are more likely to cut corners on quality when they're rushing. So what behaviors do we need to reinforce in those moments to make sure that they get it right, even under pressure?"

"That makes sense. I'd like to see if I can fit this all together. Let's take one of our indicators—clean water, for example. We can use our quadrants to understand why a person is very poor in water, and then we can identify the right behavior she needs to do in order to improve in water, based on the underlying reasons. Right?"

"Sounds to me like you're on the right path."

"And while not everyone will be very poor in water, we'll work with lots of people who are. If we build up a bank of solutions to address any given problem, we won't need to reinvent the wheel every time we work on the water indicator with someone." He nodded at me encouragingly. "But how do we move someone from problem to solution?"

"Good question. You move someone from problem to solution by making change inevitable. Change becomes inevitable when people answer 'yes' to two questions: *Is it worth it?* and *Can I do it?*" And with that, over the next few hours, he gave me an impromptu masterclass in his theory of influence.

When you look at the world through the lens of influence, you suddenly find you can start explaining things you'd always found puzzling. For example: why is it, in my country, that you're nearly twice as likely to be among the poorest of the poor than to be someone who doesn't own a smartphone? The truth is stranger than fiction: 24 percent of Paraguayans live below the national poverty line and 9 percent below the extreme poverty line, whereas only 5 percent of Paraguayans don't own a smartphone.

What smartphone companies have figured out is how to influence people's buying behavior. The behavioral nudges are everywhere. Getting cell-phone airtime is cheap and easy; you can buy it in small quantities anytime you have a little extra cash in your pocket. It's for sale at every little kiosk you pass, and even from people hawking their wares through your car window as you wait for the traffic light to turn green. So, when people ask themselves if it's possible to have a smartphone, the answer is yes. And is it valuable? Again, yes. Life is easier and life is better. The phone companies tell you this is true through aspirational advertising, your peers amplify the message, and you see it for yourself as your smartphone quickly becomes an indispensable asset. A smartphone will help you do things you couldn't do before: stay in touch with distant friends and family, access information whenever and wherever you need it, and have fun. Owning a phone bestows you with a certain amount of cachet within an increasingly materialistic society and protects you from the stigma of being one of the few people who doesn't have one.

If influence can explain why people living below the poverty line might own a smartphone, it can also explain why people living above the poverty line might not have, say, a bathroom in their home (as we've seen time and again with our clients—a fact that fairly well torpedoes the assumption, made by microfinance banks, that increased income automatically leads to increased quality of life).

So why would a poor person have a phone and a middle-class person not have a bathroom? Because there's no equivalent nudging for bathrooms. The average person in Paraguay isn't exposed to eye-catching advertisements extolling the lifestyle value of a modern hygienic bathroom on a daily basis (if at all). We don't use our bathrooms to share our vacation snaps with our cousins or show off our new bathrooms to our colleagues when we go out to dinner. We aren't reminded of the value of our bathroom every time it dings in our pocket. Likewise, the cost and complexity of installing a modern bathroom can seem daunting. Finding a trustworthy contractor, hiring a reputable plumber, sourcing affordable materials and navigating the maze of housing regulations feels impossible—and not worth it when there's no immediate gratification or social payoff involved.

I'm happy to report that *Fundación Paraguaya* did eventually crack the nut on how to build agency and self-efficacy when it comes to modern bathrooms. But before I get ahead of myself, it's worth reviewing the basic tenets of the theory of influence.

Joseph Grenny describes six sources of influence, all of which need to be activated for change to become unavoidable. According to him, we need to think about motivation (is it worth it?) and ability (can I do it?) on three levels: the personal, the social and the structural.

Motivation helps us to do things we'd rather not do, such as exercising when you'd rather be relaxing over a few episodes of *Downton Abbey* (to use an example I'm familiar with). In the absence of a nudge, it's far more likely we'll choose an option with short-term payoffs (and long-term consequences) than one with short-term consequences (and long-term payoffs). One of the things you can do to make people choose the unappealing option is to turn it into a game. Seen from this perspective, it's easy to explain why our youth-entrepreneurship training was so popular: we created personal motivation by turning a dull and unrewarding task (learning how to run a business) into a competitive sport in which students could track their progress and take pride in their achievements.

But we didn't just turn it into a sport—we turned it into a *team* sport, meaning we were also providing *social* motivation. Each student was surrounded by other students, who were all excited about the game, cheering each other on and helping each other work through the more challenging concepts. The game created instant encouragement, coaching and even accountability—if your personal success depends on your team members, you make sure everyone is pulling their weight. Structural motivation came in the form of the rewards we designed to affect the economy surrounding our students; we created rewards and prizes linked to vital behaviors. We knew, however, that external motivators have limited value—and we always relied on personal and social motivators to do their part first.

For example, we developed (together with our London-based sister organization, Teach a Man to Fish) a School Enterprise Challenge, in which students from schools across the world compete to create a sustainable business, the profits of which go toward addressing a problem in the school (fixing broken equipment, purchasing new supplies, etc.) With the support of their teachers and parents, students bake cakes, produce jam, manufacture furniture with recycled materials or sew colorful aprons for sale. They learn to identify a market niche and work as a team; raise money to purchase their inputs; create, market and sell their products; and do basic accounting to understand profit and loss. Members of the winning team are rewarded with their own tablet computer—but in reality, the game is designed to ensure everyone wins. The school benefits from the monies raised, while students take pride in supporting their school, and competing against other schools, for the chance to be represented in the finals—while having fun along the way.

When it comes to influencing behavioral changes, it seems obvious that ability has a big role to play. What I appreciate about Grenny's theory, however, is that it helps us to think about the idea of ability on three different levels (just as we can with motivation).

Personal ability is all about helping people learn new skills—and breaking the vital behaviors into smaller, bite-sized pieces that don't feel overwhelming but inevitably add up to something meaningful. Personal ability isn't just about the experience of succeeding; it's also about the experience of failing at something until you get it right. Smart influencers create an environment in which failure is safe and fear of failure (or the shame of having failed) doesn't short-circuit the learning process.

Social ability is about the value of cooperation and teamwork when we're trying to learn new skills or achieve a goal—think about how it's easier for a couple to quit smoking together, rather than just one person in the relationship quitting while the other carries on smoking.

Structural ability is about changing the environment that surrounds a person to make the right choices the easy and obvious ones to make. For someone who is dieting, this might mean going through the kitchen cupboards and replacing all the sweets with healthy snacks. For someone who is trying to quit smoking, we might suggest keeping the lighter in the car, the cigarettes in the garden shed and the ashtray in the bottom of the linen drawer so that the organizational hassle of getting ready to smoke outweighs the craving to actually do so. In short: change the space to make behavior change easy.

Over the next few months, as I continued to study Grenny's ideas, my new understanding of the science of change also helped me to see why 'magical things' were happening at our agricultural school. As it turns out, we were already using all six sources of influence on our students: building their skills in class through a game-based curriculum, giving them the facilities they needed to practice their new skills, embedding them in a supportive community, removing them from a 'low aspirations' culture they faced at home and creating financial incentives for success (such as letting them keep the profit they earned by running the campus store). This, in particular, was a real 'eureka' moment for me. Without knowing it, we'd become skilled in the art of influence. All that remained was to take all we'd learned over the past few months and inte-grate it into our new poverty methodology.

As we did so, and to our delight, we found that Grenny's theory of influence was the thing that helped us heed Wilber's warning about the importance of allowing people to climb their own ladder of awareness and development. We posi-tioned ourselves as the facilitators of change—not the drivers of change. We would empower clients to identify their depri-vations, prioritize their goals and ultimately achieve those goals. Sometimes, this would involve deliberately nudging them toward their goals; other times, it would just be about creating the conditions whereby achieving their goals would be easy and/or inevitable. It's part nudging, part influencing. The important thing is: the client climbs their own ladder, in their own way—which empowers them to keep climbing because they know it's both possible and worth it.

CHAPTER 8
POVERTY STOPLIGHT

NEARLY TWO YEARS had passed since the day when Luis Fernando challenged me to define poverty. The journey to arrive at the point where I could respond to that challenge had taken me far and wide, and deep into the communities we were serving. By October 2010, I was finally ready to give him an answer.

That didn't mean I wasn't nervous at the prospect of doing so, but at the very least, I knew we were well prepared: my team had been working diligently for five months to pull everything we'd learned into one coherent methodology, design it into a user-friendly tool and create the operational framework that would allow us to implement it. My reservation stemmed from the fact that what we'd come up with looked *nothing* like any of the other poverty tools available at the time. I had come to appreciate, and even rely on, Luis Fernando's pragmatic, skeptical nature—but I couldn't guess whether our new methodology would be a step too far in the direction of blue-sky thinking for him.

The underlying reason for my concern was that our new methodology overturns so much of what was considered 'conventional wisdom' when it came to poverty. Like so many before us, my team tried to figure out what poverty was, and how to measure it. But my conversation with Wilber had opened our eyes to the far more important question: who owns poverty? It's a deceptively simple question, and asking it leads you to a startling insight: poor people have never owned their own poverty.

To put it bluntly: poverty reduction programs are not something *done with* a community, or even *done by* a community; they are something *done to* a community—imposed from the outside when an external organization uses its own definition (however coherent), its own measures (however accurate) and its own solutions (however well-intended). A water NGO arrives and decides that water is the problem, so they build a well. An educational charity arrives and decides that schools are a problem, so they build a school. A health social enterprise arrives and decides that vaccines are the problem, so they vaccinate the kids. Please don't misunderstand me: none of these efforts are inherently a bad thing. It's just that in none of these examples is the community calling the shots, finding solutions to the problems that they themselves have articulated and prioritized. But that's not really surprising, is it? After all, if they could have, they would have already, right? (Or so the thinking goes.)

Our methodology, on the other hand, gives poverty back to poor families. First, families have *naming power* to decide what poverty means in the context of their lives. We ground the definition within the global canon of poverty literature, but the indicators we selected for our tool are those that our clients told us were important. In total, the methodology contains 50 indicators within six dimensions: 'Income and Employment', 'Health and Environment', 'Housing and Infrastructure', 'Education and Culture', 'Organization and Participation' and 'Self-Esteem and Motivation'.

Importantly, each and every indicator is framed from the perspective of the client and their family—written in the first-person plural, rather than the third-person singular. Each indicator makes the family the protagonist: *We save.*

We have diverse sources of income. We participate in the community.
Our indicators were understandable, actionable and achievable by clients themselves. Very deliberately, we created distance between ourselves and existing statistical measures of change (such as poverty indexes), which economists and social scientists conceived and created to serve policymakers and decision-makers, who need to aggregate internationally comparable data, but which bear very little relation to what's actually happening in the life of the family.

Second, the families have *judgment power* to decide where they stand, using thresholds (determined by the poor themselves) that differentiate between what it means to be very poor, poor and non-poor in each indicator.

To facilitate this, we assign a color to each state: green for non-poor, yellow for poor and red for very poor (you can guess why we starting calling it the Poverty Stoplight). Families self-diagnose their own poverty levels for each indicator by considering the pictorial representations of each state (supported by a written description and a verbal explanation from the staff member). This step amounts to what Joseph Grenny would call *making the invisible visible*, which is important because sometimes we can't see what's in front of our eyes *precisely because* we see it all the time. Some of the situations describing what it means to be 'non-poor' in certain indicators might come as a surprise to someone completing their Poverty Stoplight survey.

For instance, we found that poor people are quite capable of intuiting that clean water is important for well-being, but might not appreciate the importance of having that running clean water near their house and always available (because, after all, human beings are perfectly capable of adapting to less-than-optimal situations). Or they might vote but not understand the value of knowing how to petition the government for public services. What the Poverty Stoplight does is to name all of the distinct faces of poverty at once, in a way that is comprehensive, easy to understand and visible—all in one place and one moment. And the client, for the first time, has a visual record of their own personal poverty—a large, sturdy card with 50 colored dots describing their situation in relation to each indicator; where they're doing well, and where they can make improvements.

When it comes to eliminating poverty, we also learned that celebrating each family's strengths is just as important as naming their weaknesses. It allows them to, as the axiom says, 'count their blessings, or else they don't count'. This allows families to see how apparently insignificant little details in life can affect other, seemingly more important things—for example, by connecting self-esteem (a soft indicator) with income-generating capacity (a hard indicator).

When a family has detailed, easy-to-understand data about their poverties and non-poverties all in one place, they can also start to recalibrate their relationship with the word 'poverty'. Much like we (as a Foundation) have moved away from a simple reductionist definition of 'poor equals living on less than $2 a day', time and again we've heard poor families, after taking the visual survey, exclaim that they're not as poor as they thought they were. They cry: "Is that all it is? Oh, in that case, I can do something about it!" (In a similar vein, we've heard members of the so-called middle class exclaim, after taking the visual survey, that they're poorer than they thought they were—on which more later.)

The final piece of the puzzle is about ensuring that families have the *action power* to do something about the various deprivations they've identified in their lives. That's why the methodology includes a Life Map. Once a family assigns a color to each indicator, the facilitator starts a conversation about which five indicators are the family's top priorities to tackle first. If you think about poverty as an ear of corn, the Poverty Stoplight simply breaks poverty down into bite-sized kernels.

For each priority area, the family reflects on three questions: *Why don't I have it?* (drawing from Wilber's quadrants), *What can I do to attain it?* (drawing from Grenny's six sources of influence) and *When will I have it?* (creating a realistic timeframe to take concrete steps toward an achievable goal). All of this information is recorded directly into the Life Map, which the family keeps for reference. Our role in all of this is activating the family's agency (potential energy) to eliminate their own poverty in the areas they prioritize, leveraging all six sources of influence to help them along the way.

Having actionable indicators that families can directly influence is important here. If the idea of poverty seems too abstract, or if a family feels too alienated from the root causes of their poverty, then the path of least resistance will always be inaction. But once a family can see the small concrete steps they can take to improve their life, that's a really powerful motivator. Suddenly, it's all clear. Suddenly, it's all within reach. *It's worth it, and I can achieve it.* What is more, they have a mentor, who has access to a bank of solutions that correspond to the reason for and severity of the family's unique deprivation.

You'll notice I'm using the word 'family', rather than 'person', as my unit of analysis. There's a reason for this, and it's a lesson we learned through our work with our microfinance clients. None of us live our lives in isolation, and we share resources within families in response to challenges and opportunities and to harness economies of scale.

I am certainly aware of the practical limitations and drawbacks of focusing on families rather than individuals. I know our work comes in for criticism from social scientists who would rather the unit of observation and analysis (the 'what' and the 'who') to be the individual. I know others will criticize our approach because inequities within families become less visible if the unit of analysis is the family. Also, there is a legitimate concern that a lack of a functioning family unit might often be the thing creating poverty (e.g. homeless people, orphans).

Despite these things, we find it more practical to use family household (the people who sleep and eat under one same roof) as our unit of analysis because society is made up of communities, which are made of families. Family groups are essential for survival and well-being. Families serve to transmit culture from one generation to another. Families provide support in times of failure and celebration in times of successes. Healthy families produce healthy individuals.

We have also come to learn that there are usually idle resources at the family level. What's more: families need to work together to eliminate poverty, and that starts with both a common understanding of the problem and a shared motivation to do something about it. Take, for example, Ana Maria from the town of Ybicuí. She needed to move from yellow to green in the 'Diversified Sources of Income' indicator. Noting that Ana Maria's 22-year-old son was at home during the day, the Loan Officer asked her why he wasn't working. Ana Maria said he studied rural management at college every night from 6pm to 9pm. In discussing how he could leverage his free time to contribute to the family's income, they decided he would take on a cleaning supplies microfranchise (a Foundation program), selling door to door in the area.

For us, as a development organization, talking about poor families rather than poor people also opens up interesting possibilities. First, it changes the scale of the problem. In practice, we no longer work with only 70,000 microfinance clients; we are supporting 70,000 families. At a rate of 4.5 members per family, this means we are trying to guide 315,000 people out of poverty. In other words, one organization stands to make a significant contribution, given the right tools. This logic works both ways. If we look at Paraguay, we don't have 7 million inhabitants but rather 1.4 million family households. This might seem like a sleight of hand, but it's worth considering that the perceived size of the challenge has a direct and inverse relationship to our confidence that we can rise to it.

Perhaps more importantly, naming families as the unit of analysis opens the door to a whole new level of coordination between development agencies and organizations working to alleviate poverty. Some of those organizations only vaccinate children; some only provide business-management training to women; some only boost agricultural entrepreneurship skills among men. Yet none of these efforts unfold in a vacuum. Healthier kids mean the mother has more time to devote to work; a more business-savvy wife can effectively sell her husband's produce at market; a more effective farmer will grow more, better and more diverse crops, which boosts sales and contributes to better household nutrition. You'd be hard-pressed to throw a stone in a developing country and not hit a development NGO—and just because the left hand doesn't know what the right hand is doing doesn't mean they don't all share the same goal. If we expect families to come together to tackle the problem of poverty, shouldn't the same apply to all the organizations out there working to eliminate poverty?

And yes, I really am using the word 'eliminate'. We're not aiming to simply reduce poverty to some arbitrary level that we perceive to be morally acceptable or realistically achievable. We don't want to merely alleviate its effects, like a doctor who cures the symptoms but ignores the disease. What's more, 'reduce' and 'alleviate' are such elastic, ambiguous and diffuse ideas; no one really knows what they mean – how much poverty reduction is *enough* poverty reduction – which means we have no idea how to even begin putting them into practice.

And this, it must be said, was the first concern Luis Fernando raised when we sat down together to review the draft tool. He didn't waste time getting to the point: "Don't you think that poverty is too intractable, too complex for an organization such as ours to do anything about it? Especially in a country as poor as ours."

"It might not seem obvious at first," I said, "but using 50 indicators to describe poverty is actually much simpler than using only one indicator, such as income, or an index comprised of ten different indicators. Yes, there are a lot of different things that come together to influence whether or not we're poor: our country's systems, our culture, our own actions, our beliefs, our aspirations. But there's nothing inherently wrong with complexity. We just need the right tools to help us transform complexity from a challenge into an opportunity. Think of the Poverty Stoplight as being able to genetically sequence an individual family's poverty. Once you can do that, you can create personalized poverty-elimination medicine.

"Let's imagine two different families living in the same community," I continued. "One is poor in water, the other is not. What does this tell us? First, it tells us that water poverty is not inevitable in that community, because there is at least one family beating the odds. Furthermore, it means that the water-poor family can learn from the water non-poor family—because just like we pool knowledge and resources within families, we do the same within communities. But all those insights and resources about how to be non-poor will lie dormant until we know how to deploy them in any given community. If we were using some index to describe families in terms of poverty percentages or income brackets, we couldn't do any of that."

"So, what will this do to our institutional goals?" he asked.

"Our current goals are to increase family income, strengthen precarious jobs and create new jobs. This new tool will let us go farther, deeper, than that. We'll be able to embrace the concept of poverty elimination. Now, with this concrete and measurable strategy, everyone knows exactly what success looks like, what the end of poverty means: to work on your reds and yellows, and to eventually be green in everything. From a management point of view, it's great. We know what to measure, we know how to measure it and we know when we've got the job done."

"But how dare we ask a stranger about their latrine or even their self-esteem?"

"Ah, you see, we're not," I replied. "That's the whole point. It is not I, nor our Loan Officer, nor any social worker who conducts the interview. It is the poor person, the head of the poor household, who self-diagnoses their own level of poverty. Neither you nor I have the capacity or the confidence to ask a stranger whether, for example, she feels she has enough autonomy to make decisions in her home. But she does."

"But the poor, uneducated people we are dealing with will have no capacity to understand the data. How will we manage the data? How will we put forth this information so that policymakers can make some sense out of it?"

"Why do you believe that policymakers are the only decision-makers when it comes to a family's poverty? The mother of a teenager girl has a profound influence on whether her daughter will finish high school, or whether she will get pregnant and drop out of school. Everybody knows that. The prime user of the data produced by the self-diagnosis is the head of the household. She doesn't need some complex poverty index of aggregated data in a spreadsheet telling her about abstract things like percentages or change over time. She needs targeted information: my family has these three reds and those six yellows. Nine things to work on to be green in everything."

"So, on top of the fact that they are poor, you are going to burden them with getting themselves out of poverty?" he asked. "Isn't that a little cruel?"

"Don't underestimate people just because they might be poor in some ways, because they're rich in other ways. The most important consequence of the Poverty Stoplight is that, by allowing the poor to self-diagnose and measure their level of poverty, they are empowered to own their poverty, and do something about it. We're not giving them anything that they can't actually do—we know that everything is within their reach, because they defined the indicators, and because if they're red or yellow in an indicator, they probably know someone who is green who they can learn from.

"And anyway, owning their own poverty doesn't mean that poor families are left to fend for themselves," I continued. "That's why we created a dimension called 'Organization and Participation'. In this category, we included action-able indicators such as being part of a self-help group, having the capacity to influence the public sector, having problem-solving abilities, and being registered voters and voting in elections. Getting your family out of poverty means that families are encouraged not only to help themselves but also to become active seekers of solutions—citizen activists capable of signing petitions and staging protests so that government service providers become aware of their needs and are held accountable for meeting them. We all know that, if demand is not articulated, it is easy for poor people to become invisible. And it's not just governments that will benefit from more visible poverty. The Poverty Stoplight will allow development organizations to deploy their own resources more efficiently. Not everyone in a community will be red in health—so not everyone needs health education. Not everyone in a community will be red in literacy—so not everyone needs literacy education. But without knowing who needs what, we tend to apply blanket, one-size-fits-all solutions to any given problem."

"You say things like health and education, and that's what worries me," Luis Fernando said. "We don't do any of those things. *Fundación Paraguaya* is in the business of enterprise loans. It's *quid pro quo*. We provide loans, and clients pay them back. If we start dabbling in this poverty stuff, then they'll start thinking that we're one of those charities that offer free services—like the ones that go to the slums and hand out free wheelchairs or eyeglasses. It would be sending mixed signals—and then clients won't pay back their loans because they think they are a gift. Or, they'll tell us they can't repay because they suddenly have realized that they need a modern bathroom. And what about the burden on our Loan Officers? To tell them that they have to do their job *and* get people out of poverty? We can't do it."

"I hear your concerns. I do. All I can say is that we've been trying this visual survey out with clients, and they love it. They've never been asked these kinds of questions before, and the whole thing is eye-opening. What's more, clients are really embracing it, taking charge. It's not a burden, it's an awakening. One client pointed to her completed survey and said 'That's it? Poverty is nothing more than this? I've been living in the slums all my life. I started working at 13, and I got pregnant with my first child at 14. And now I have a roadmap to get out of poverty. I never thought that I could do it, but now I see that it's easy.'"

"But that's my point—getting out of poverty isn't easy!" he retorted. "What happens to that woman when she is green in everything? She'll still be living the slums. She'll still be relatively uneducated. What makes you think that her life will be any different?"

"Her life will be different because she'll be a slum dweller who is non-poor. It's an important distinction, but maybe one that's difficult to understand. She won't be rich, she won't have an extravagant lifestyle and her life won't be without challenges. But she'll have joined the Paraguayan middle class—and when I say that I'm not talking about income levels or type of profession. Being a member of the middle class is nothing more than being able to ask for what you want. To demand your rights. To set goals and work toward them, because you know they're worth achieving, and because you know that you can. It's about no longer accepting a status quo that doesn't meet your needs simply because you can't imagine life any other way. Once she's green in everything, she'll take it from there. Once she's activated, she'll keep going. We're just helping her through the hardest part."

Luis Fernando nodded. I could tell that he still had his doubts, but he seemed willing to suspend judgment for the moment. As for myself, I was amused by two things. One, that over the course of researching and designing the Poverty Stoplight, the all-powerful income indicator – money – had become just one of the family's priorities, and not always the most important one (a point that would take us a few years to fully appreciate). Two, I saw the irony implicit in the fact that, having gone abroad to do undergraduate and graduate studies in how to create national development plans, here I was helping to create *family* development plans based on their own poverty dashboard. I had moved from the macro the micro—and I had never been more certain that I was on the right path.

CHAPTER 9
ACCEPTANCE

GIVEN THE HEAT OF OUR MIDDAY SUN, it's not unusual to get an early start on the day—and for business trading hours to continue long into the evening. And so it was that at eight o'clock on a bright spring morning I arrived at a small, two-bedroom house with a big, shady garden belonging to a microfinance client. With her husband having long since left for work, and her children already at school, she'd busied herself cleaning the house and opening her small kiosk before sitting down to talk with her *Fundación Paraguaya* Loan Officer. Her Loan Officer, armed with paper files and a clipboard, was there to conduct a Poverty Stoplight visual survey. Luis Fernando and I were present, along with the Regional Manager, to witness the process.

All other things being equal, this should have been a triumphant day for me. Two years of hard work with a small and dedicated team had culminated in the creation of our new methodology to diagnose and eliminate poverty. As I walked him through the theory underlying the Poverty Stoplight, Luis Fernando had seemed satisfied with what he was hearing, even if he wasn't without his doubts. When he'd left my office, I'd felt buoyant. Today, he'd be seeing it in action for the very first time. I was nervous, of course. One of Luis Fernando's rare qualities is his split-screen brain: he can focus on the strategic big picture and fine operational details at the very same time. This very thing makes him both formidable and invaluable at the helm of the Foundation— and meant nothing that happened that morning would go unnoticed.

We looked on as the Loan Officer showed the client a series of color-coded illustrations on paper and asked her to identify which she felt represented her status in each indicator. The very process of doing the survey created a space for a new and profound conversation between the client and her Loan Officer. Together, they discussed the details of the woman's life; her family's accomplishments and challenges. It was potentially the first time she'd ever been encouraged to reflect on different aspects of her life, and to call out her challenges, in that way. By visualizing what success looked like in each indicator, the woman had (also, perhaps, for the first time) a tangible picture of what was possible—in health, in water, in teeth, in community participation. She had a concrete direction for her aspiration; a picture of what it meant to be 'not poor'.

What's more, because she identified her own status in each indicator, that information *belonged* to the woman. She *owned* it. She was also the first person to see the results of her survey—rather than having them be whisked away to some data entry assistant in the head office. As soon as the visual survey was complete and her card was filled with colored dots, she worked with her Loan Officer to transform it into a Life Map—her very own, unique, self-directed family poverty-elimination plan.

To begin, they made a list of the woman's principal accomplishments—her green indicators. This might sound like an odd place to start, especially when faced with a survey littered with reds and yellows, all competing for attention. But as much as we don't want to reduce poverty to a lack of money, we also don't want to reduce the Life Map to a series of deprivations. By encouraging people to count their blessings, to honor the ways in which they'd beaten the odds (despite all the structural, economic, political and cultural factors creating and perpetuating their poverty), we start each and every conversation about poverty elimination from a position of strength and abundance, rather than with a scarcity mindset. We are all rich in our own ways, after all.

Next, the woman prioritized which of the red or yellow indicators she would work on in the next 12 months, and (importantly, as we'd learned from Wilber), together with the Loan Officer, reflected on the probable reasons behind these deprivations so they could identify the right solution. For example, a woman might prioritize improving her health indicator—but there's no use in giving her the phone number of the local clinic if it's fear that's keeping her away.

Then, having defined the woman's specific and measurable mini-goals and desired results, the Loan Officer and client brainstormed ideas on how to meet those goals. As Grenny suggested, the coaching process focused on behaviors. They identified friends or neighbors who manage to beat the odds in a given indicator (positive deviants), and who could serve as role models in this indicator. They also defined vital behaviors and crucial moments—when decisions should be made and actions must be taken to accomplish her goals. Finally, they studied *Fundación Paraguaya's* inventory of locally tested solutions and agreed on next steps. If the survey helped her to break the question of poverty down into small, bite-sized chunks, the Life Map helped her to break those chunks down into even smaller, highly manageable tasks.

In this instance, the woman began to see that she could venture into neighboring slums to sell her merchandise— something that never occurred to her. She learned that she could go to the Ministry of Public Works and ask for help in fixing the neighborhood's damaged bridge—and that she was not limited to dealing with the (relatively ineffective) local municipality. At the end of the session, the client, aided by her Loan Officer, developed an action plan. Tasks ranged from personal activities (expanding her business trade routes) to indirect activities (starting a petition over the need for bridge repairs).

It had all gone perfectly to plan, without a hitch. The Loan Officer had acquitted herself excellently; the client had been animated and engaged throughout. I was sure the whole exercise helped the Loan Officer and the client connect in a way they never had before. I imagined my colleagues were feeling much the same as I was in that moment. Brimming with enthusiasm, I chatted casually with the client as the Loan Officer left for her next meeting—but Luis Fernando pulled me to one side, asking for a moment to speak with me and the Regional Manager together.

I readily agreed, and started by congratulating the Regional Manager on the professionalism with which his Loan Officer conducted the Poverty Stoplight.

"That might be so, but she is really upset," Luis Fernando interjected. "The process takes too long. The Poverty Stoplight takes an hour and a half to apply, sometimes two hours. Then, she must go to the office and manually input all the data into her computer. How can you ask this of our Loan Officers? They have a basic salary, and earn commission on the number of loan disbursements, number of clients and delinquency rates. The Loan Officer we met today, for example, needs to meet eight clients today. Because of how long these interviews take, she'll only get to see four. She'll miss her target by half. While you were chatting with the client, she complained to the Regional Manager. As it stands, we both believe that we will soon have a mutiny among our Loan Officers. I recommend that we suspend the Poverty Stoplight, with immediate effect."

I was floored. I had heard Luis Fernando's concerns yesterday, but was convinced they would be moot once he saw the Poverty Stoplight in action. At least in my mind, it was clear we were onto something important, and to abandon our efforts now seemed an act of lunacy.

Had I been listening closely, I'd have heard a sentiment that I would hear time and again—and still hear today: *it's not possible, and it's not worth it.* Conventional wisdom holds that poverty is too big, hairy and complicated to defeat. The odds are against us. Don't even bother.

I've never been one for conventional wisdom, but looking back I can see that I could have done a better job in influencing those around me on the question of the Poverty Stoplight. With any type of organizational change, one meets a certain amount of initial resistance. It's not that Luis Fernando didn't believe in our mission—I knew he did. It's that all he saw was the additional work, without having any real-life experience of the potential benefits. Had I been clever, I would have used Grenny's theory of influence to lead an effective process of organizational change, focusing on the questions of motivation and ability within individuals, groups and systems. I'm sorry to admit that I used the management equivalent of brute force to move forward with the project. For the second time, I pulled rank on Luis Fernando. It was a tense stand-off, but I overruled him on principle.

I asked him to roll out the Poverty Stoplight on a limited basis—not with all our clients, but with a small subset of them. Each Loan Officer would get to choose which clients to work with, meaning they could target the 'low-hanging fruit' first. Their goal was to help 10 percent of their clients become green in income and 5 percent green in everything. By starting with the easy clients, and only a handful of them, I was convinced staff would quickly get to grips with how to use the Poverty Stoplight, and come to appreciate its value. After all, we already had training modules on many of the indicators—savings, family budgeting and others. But instead, the onus was on the Loan Officer to not only deliver training but also make sure the desired behavior change was actually happening (and, indeed, we would soon be shocked to learn just how few of our clients were using family budgets as they'd been taught). In return, I promised Luis Fernando we would try to come up with some sort of computerized version of the Poverty Stoplight that would save everyone time and effort.

Until then, and during those 'low-hanging fruit' years, we didn't change any of the staff incentives or targets; I just added to their workload and hoped for the best. I had no idea what was going to happen—and it could very well have all gone horribly wrong. All the while, I was bracing myself for the staff revolt that Luis Fernando had predicted. But when it eventually happened, it was for a completely different reason.

THREE MONTHS LATER, in January 2011, at the World Economic Forum meeting in Davos, Switzerland, I was running late. I was meant to be joining a Schwab Foundation for Social Entrepreneurship breakfast workshop at a venue that was, ostensibly, right next to my hotel. I thought it would take me 10 minutes to get there. It took me 25. When I arrived – out of breath and kicking myself for being late for the most important meeting I'd have all year – dozens of people were already paired off and engrossed in the kind of conversation I desperately needed to be having right then.

The event was a meeting of minds from two sectors: tech companies and social entrepreneurs. At the time, tech companies were waking up to the importance of sustainability and social impact, and social entrepreneurs were starting to get an inkling of how technology could help them scale. I was a social entrepreneur with a tech problem. But how was

I going to find someone to help me solve that problem when everyone was already deep in dialogue?

That's when serendipity walked in—in the shape of Paul Ellingstad from Hewlett-Packard (HP). He burst into the room, similarly out of breath, and we shared a laugh about our tardiness. As the only loners in the room, we decided to grab a table and start talking. Paul started off by telling me about the HP Office of Sustainability and Social Innovation. They wanted to find a way to use technology to reduce suffering in the world, and were looking to team up with an organization doing social-change work on the ground. I told him about *Fundación Paraguaya* and the challenge of turning a paper tool into a tech tool. He smiled and asked to see more. I opened my bag and arranged on the table in front of us a paper copy of the interview guide, a color-coded sample Poverty Stoplight and a sample Life Map.

"The Poverty Stoplight is a visual survey, and frames the interview process between staff and clients. It's structured so they can focus on a defined set of indicators that are described in both words and pictures, so it's user-friendly even for illiterate clients. Together, these indicators represent multidimensional poverty in our country. But right now, it takes too long. We need our methodology to be practical, time- and cost-effective, convenient and easy to use."

"So, who manages your visual survey? Who fills out the questionnaire?" he asked.

"Our Loan Officer has a very active role during the visual survey through dialogue. She provides clarifying information so that the client can better answer each indicator. Ultimately, however, it is the client who chooses the color that represents her status and marks the card accordingly."

"So, this information is only for client use?" he asked.

"It's first and foremost for her, but we can also use it to guide our interventions. We can create personalized training and mentoring programs for each family, and provide integrated microfinance services such as credit, savings and insurance. But it's not just about what solutions we can deliver. The information also helps us make an inventory of local solutions for each indicator. In this way, we can link demand with the supply of social services. We have started creating partnerships and alliances with various government organizations, civil society organizations and private companies that can provide basic services to our clients, above and beyond the financial services or training that we ourselves can provide."

"Okay. That makes sense. Do you have any thoughts about how technology can help you do all that?"

""I might. It would be great if we could use some sort of tablet or laptop to implement the Poverty Stoplight visual survey. The paper version just takes too long, and it's not even done once we leave the house of the client. Staff have to go back to the office and input every answer into an Excel spreadsheet by hand, which takes a lot of time to do and to check. Have you ever heard of SurveyMonkey? It's this online survey thing. Maybe we could turn the Poverty Stoplight into a SurveyMonkey—what do you think?"

He smiled at me—perhaps out of kindness, or perhaps out of bemusement at hearing such a rudimentary suggestion. "How about I do you one better?" he asked.

And he did. One year later, we unveiled the first generation of our tablet-based visual survey. It was beautiful. It allowed us to capture data instantly, even when we were working without access to the internet; store that data in the cloud; geo-reference each survey, so we could create community poverty maps; photograph the families and their houses; create a baseline for repeat surveys with families; and aggregate data, so we could have color-coded community poverty graphs. Clients were eager to use the tablet system and found it easy regardless of their level of literacy. But the most important thing the technology did was create the conditions that would allow us to push the boundaries of possibility with the Poverty Stoplight. We could aggregate the data up, to create community-level solutions; and we could disaggregate the data down, to focus on family-level solutions.

I am deeply appreciative of the time and support HP gave us, and that they provided the technology and the platform free of cost. I am also aware, however, that it might have taken less time, and been a smoother process, had I not personally been involved. The truth was that I was leading an initiative I didn't understand (and not for the first time, having started *Fundación Paraguaya* with approximately zero knowledge on banking and finance). Naming SurveyMonkey as a model for what 'success' looked like should have given Paul a clear indication of what he was dealing with from the start of our collaboration. I struggled to keep up when he talked about things such as 'cloud storage' and 'secure data transmission'. I didn't know what he meant by terms like 'graphic user interface' and 'API' (I still don't). That I didn't know how to articulate what I needed was down to the fact that I didn't know what was even possible. By asking smart questions about how we were working, who we wanted to use this poverty data and how, Paul was able to anticipate a lot of our needs. In fact, as early as our second phone call, he very astutely (and gently) asked me to bring our head of information technology into the conversation; he simply wasn't getting anywhere with me.

As fruitful as our collaboration was, it was doomed to be short-lived. By 2015, HP split into two companies and Paul's office dissolved. We had worked together to create the first visual survey platform, and kept iterating once we put it into the hands of staff. We translated the survey from paper into digital and incorporated a geo-tagging function. Survey data was immediately added to the database and survey results were automatically generated, so we had individual and aggregate results in real time. In 2016, with the support of the Skoll Foundation, we started working with other developers to produce the next generation of the visual survey. This time, we wanted the platform to be open source, so that anyone could download it, improve it and share it with the rest of the user community.

MEANWHILE, Foundation staff had been busy rolling out the paper version of the Poverty Stoplight—each with approximately 50 clients. We made it clear to clients from the outset that the Poverty Stoplight didn't change our relationship with them in any way. We would still provide loans to clients perceived as unbankable, and in return we would expect them to continue repaying us faithfully. The Poverty Stoplight isn't charity; it's a self-assessment. If a client is red in the 'Kitchen Stove' indicator, we're not going to give them a stove—much like a hungry person can't walk into a restaurant and receive food for free. We were fortunate that this message fell on good ears—and fortunate, too, that clients seemed to embrace the project with eagerness. It's easy to imagine that a person could feel overwhelmed or depressed when they come face to face with a detailed catalog of their deprivations, but instead our clients took ownership of their Poverty Stoplights—even to the point that they would proudly display their Stoplight in their home or kiosk.

As clients embraced responsibility for overcoming their deprivations, our Loan Officers were embracing the task of creating a catalog of solutions to help clients tackle their red and yellow indicators. While they were starting this catalog from scratch, we were certain they could do it, because (by design) all of the indicators are understandable, actionable and achievable by clients themselves.

The enthusiasm and initiative shown by the whole team were gratifying; for the first time, it felt like the Poverty Stoplight could be a real game-changer for *Fundación*

Paraguaya. Which is why, I'll be honest, I was completely surprised when the rumbling started. Quiet murmurs, building into whispered conversations, crescendoing into frank talks between Loan Officers and Office Managers, between Office Managers and Regional Managers, between Regional Managers and Luis Fernando. By the time Luis Fernando came to me with the news, it seemed we had on our hands the staff mutiny he had so astutely foreseen.

CHAPTER 10
CREDIBILITY

IF ACHIEVING SCALE WAS A LOCKED DOOR, the visual survey software was the key that allowed us to open it. Moving away from the paper survey meant we could apply the tool to hundreds of thousands of clients quickly and easily, without having to worry about data input, storage or security. Loan Officers could apply the digital survey in a third of the time it took to apply the paper survey. The head office could instantly view data aggregated by office, region or even Loan Officer. We could create neighborhood 'poverty heat maps' that showed the distribution of each deprivation in terms of severity. Just imagine what we – what everyone in the development industry – could do with such powerful information at our fingertips. I felt sure that the Poverty Stoplight, and our coaching methodology, put the goal of eliminating global poverty within our grasp for the first time.

Here was the catch: the numbers were not on our side. By 2013, *Fundación Paraguaya* had 108 field staff and 57,485 clients. Even taking into consideration an average family size of 5, and that Loan Officers only applied the Stoplight to 12.5 percent of their clients, we were only reaching 7,207 families with our poverty-elimination methodology—which worked out as 1.7 percent of income-poor families in Paraguay. Even if we worked at full steam, and applied the Stoplight to each and every client, we'd only be able to reach 13 percent of poor families nationally. And, when you looked at our actual and potential outreach in relation to the number of poor families across the entire world, our work would never be more than a very small drop in a very large ocean of need.

Teaming up with other organizations to implement the Poverty Stoplight visual survey and coaching methodology – within Paraguay, the region and the world – seemed the logical next step. There was one catch. We needed to prove it actually worked and did what it was designed to do: provide households with an accurate picture of their multidimensional poverty, and activate them to overcome their deprivations. We needed to join the ranks of 'credible poverty-measurement methodologies', and to do so we needed to conclusively prove it was reliable, valid, practical and powerful. In plain English, that meant we needed to answer the following questions: Does it produce the same results when applied twice to the same family? Does it produce the same results as a different (already proven) test applied to the same family? Is it too difficult, complex or costly to apply? Does it produce information that is useful to a variety of stakeholders?

At that point, we'd only ever tried to answer the all-important question of whether the methodology worked in the most informal of ways. Our own institutional data (which we had, thanks to the new tablet-driven system), as well as countless conversations with clients, revealed that there is usually a positive and consistent trend in poverty reduction—meaning that, across repeated applications of the visual survey, the number of reds and yellows decreased over time and the number of greens increased. As promising as this might have seemed, however, it was only anecdotal evidence; from an academic perspective, it was 'interesting' but not 'convincing'.

We needed to do rigorous research into the Poverty Stoplight methodology—to test it, to apply statistical analysis to our data, and to put the results in front of some of the best minds in social impact assessment to see whether it could hold its own in the pantheon of globally accepted poverty-measurement tools.

So, I did what anyone in my situation would have done: I went off to get a PhD at Tulane University. More to the point: to *finish* my PhD, which I had started years earlier but never completed. Until then, I had always viewed my doctoral studies as a personal project that would allow me to teach online courses at foreign universities, but over time other priorities took precedence. Suddenly, however, those studies took on a new significance: an untapped resource that would help me achieve my goal of proving (and improving) the Poverty Stoplight.

A word of caution before I launch into a detailed discussion on my research methods and findings. If you're allergic to, on in any way wary of, detailed discussions of research methods and findings, might I gently suggest you skip ahead to the next chapter? I've tried to provide you, dear reader, with a brief plain-English rundown, but I also acknowledge that this chapter isn't going to be everyone's cup of tea. That being said, no story of the development of the Poverty Stoplight would be complete without including this experience—so here goes.

ON A SUNNY SPRING MORNING in October 2015 in a small rural village in Paraguay called Colonia 4000, close to our regional office of Santaní, 32 men and women sat around six tables in a shady garden, chatting informally with our local staff. This community of 200 households shared similar characteristics with those to whom we provided our microfinance services, and thus was an ideal place for our work.

We were there to conduct a series of exercises called Participatory Wealth Ranking (PWR). The PWR is an ingenious tool, created by social scientists, which allows members of a community to define what 'poor', 'very poor' and 'non-poor' mean in that community, and then assign a poverty category to each household and record the information on a map. Much in the way that we had designed the Poverty Stoplight based on these kinds of conversations, the PWR resulted in a hyper-local definition of poverty, based on community engagement and consensus. The key difference is that the Poverty Stoplight used this sort of process to create a standardized set of indicators to be used across all villages in a country, whereas the PWR could produce different definitions in different villages based on input from community members.

In small groups, participants discussed and agreed their poverty definition, and then used it to rank each of the community's 200 families according to their relative household wealth. By mixing up the groups and repeating this exercise a few times, we came up with a consensus of who were the 24 wealthiest households in the village, and who were the 24 poorest households in the village.

Once we had this information in hand, we tasked our local Loan Officers with visiting each of those 48 households to conduct the Poverty Stoplight visual survey, so that we could determine whether the Poverty Stoplight results lined up with the PWR results. By carrying out a few straightforward statistical tests, I would be able to ascertain whether there was a significant difference between the average poverty of the two PWR groups, and whether the poor households (according to the PWR) were also consistently poor according to the Poverty Stoplight, and vice versa. This would suggest a strong criterion-related validity for the Poverty Stoplight when compared to an existing 'gold standard' poverty-measurement tool.

While the results showed a high level of correlation between the Stoplight and the PWR, the PWR tool is deeply community-specific. Therefore, any correlation between Poverty Stoplight and the PWR results would only be valid for that one specific community in that one moment in time. We'd need to carry out similar comparative studies in other communities to see if the relationship would hold, but at least we were off to a good start. Also, since neither the Poverty Stoplight nor the PWR has a multidimensional poverty threshold, both tools were useful for ranking the situations of households in relation to each other but limited in their capacity to discriminate between households that were poor or non-poor in absolute terms. Despite this, I felt encouraged to tackle the many other research questions that lay ahead of me.

THE QUESTION OF RELIABILITY came next. To study this, we applied the Poverty Stoplight visual survey twice, with a two-week gap in between applications, to the same group of 325 women (using the same Loan Officers each time) to ascertain whether the results of the test and the re-test would match. We couldn't guard against the possibility of a family changing their answer between applications, either as a result of having taken the survey or because of an actual change in their circumstances in the two-week period. However, we could limit the effects of recall by withholding the first set of results from the family. Likewise, we asked our Loan Officers not to complete the Life Map part of the process until after the second application of the visual survey.

The results indicated that the Poverty Stoplight is, in fact, reliable—inasmuch as a repeated application of the visual survey tool leads to the same measurement outcome, both overall and within each indicator. However, one issue I found related to the scale on which the Poverty Stoplight is based. Having only three levels restricts the level of variability of the scale, allowing small changes to have a large effect in statistical tests. If there was a desire to run more complex statistical tests, the scales of the Poverty Stoplight's indicators would need to be expanded. But then again, having more levels of the scale would mean we'd need to drop the three-color scheme—which would make the tool less compelling, more difficult to grasp and somehow less motivational. Given that the primary user of the tool is the family, this seemed an acceptable trade-off to make.

VALIDITY TESTS look at whether the Poverty Stoplight accurately measures what it claims to measure. In other words, did the indicators we chose (out of all possible indicators in the universe that we *could have* chosen) give a complete picture of poverty, and was the way we defined the thresholds within each indicator accurate?

To get at this question, I conducted a series of focus-group discussions on the visual survey with clients, non-clients, staff and local poverty experts to find out whether the Poverty Stoplight seemed valid to those being tested, those using the tool, those that had already used the tool and those seeing the tool for the first time. The results of these discussions (around something called *face validity*) were encouraging, but by no means the end of the road in terms of my research.

A related test was whether the logic of the visual survey held up when I surveyed people without any reference to the tool itself (called *logical validity*). If the face validity interviews were about putting all the pieces together and seeing if they made sense (on the face of things), this test was about reverse engineering poverty to see if what we came up with matched the tool. For this reason, I held another round of focus-group discussions and semi-structured interviews with clients, non-clients, local poverty experts and government officials to ask: What does poverty mean to you? How can we eliminate it? Whose responsibility is it to eliminate poverty?

Based on the responses, I found that poverty definitions between clients and non-clients were broadly similar—unsurprising, given that they came from similar communities and socioeconomic conditions. Poverty, to them, meant not having a good quality of life, which depended on whether a family had certain conditions or deprivations. The primary concern for both of these groups was the availability of work. Other deprivations mentioned were housing, appropriate clothing, health care, nourishment, hygiene, education, training, basic rights and access to opportunities.

When asked whose responsibility it was to address poverty, clients and non-clients believed the government had an important role, because it was responsible for addressing one of the most important aspects of poverty: providing access to stable employment, income and opportunities (in the form of access to education). However, clients and non-clients also believed individuals had responsibility for addressing their own deprivations, through hard work and determination—which, in turn, required self-esteem. Problems of individual motivation were described as habits of conformism, indulging in vices or being stuck in their situation or in poverty. As one client from the town of Santaní insisted: "Some people work hard every day, but there are also people who don't want to fight. And that's the difference: if you stay at home sitting around, drinking *terere*, you're not going to get anything, you're not going to get ahead."

Moreover, the people I interviewed identified the family as a source of support. A lack of a supportive family was considered a weakness for poor people, as it represented abandonment and destitution. At the same time, my interviewees showed a strong sense of responsibility toward their families. Many women saw their children as a source of motivation for overcoming poverty, saying they wanted to provide their children with a better life than they had, and also criticized young people when they demonstrated a lack of interest in studying or working hard.

The experts I interviewed focused mainly on the concept of opportunity – in the form of access to education, training, nutrition, health and housing – and that the responsibility for overcoming poverty lay with both individuals and the government. Self-esteem and motivation were identified as important drivers for overcoming poverty and the feeling of being 'stuck'. They also discussed the need for stability (in terms of income and employment), and its effect on one's ability to plan and take risks. In addition to a positive mental outlook, experts thought assets played a central role in poverty – including having a clean bathroom, a modern kitchen, appropriate clothing, savings, access to health care and food – and that the role of the government centered around helping people with access to these assets.

I compared these definitions to the Poverty Stoplight's definition of poverty to determine whether the Stoplight contained all the elements considered important by those living in (or near) poverty, as well as those studying poverty. Their spontaneous responses matched 22 of my Poverty Stoplight indicators (out of 50 in total). However, it's also true that some of the specific Stoplight indicators were implied by the general poverty concepts mentioned during my interviews. For example, education was identified as being very important. In this case, although not specifically mentioned, I assume that our indicators 'We Know How to Read and Write', 'Children in Schooling up to 12th Grade' and 'School Supplies' would also be considered important, as they are closely related to education. Conversely, respondents mentioned seven poverty indicators that are not contained in the Poverty Stoplight, including: consumption of drugs and alcohol, a sense of responsibility toward family, spirituality, retirement planning, interaction with local businesses and NGOs, and labor migration. Finally, a few indicators were not spontaneously mentioned during interviews, nor can they be assumed to fit within a general definition. For example, the Stoplight indicator 'Access to Information' (via radio and TV) was never specifically mentioned in any interview. However, given the small number of these, the results suggest that the Poverty Stoplight has logical validity because its indicators generally line up with the definition of poverty, as given by clients, non-clients and external experts.

Another aspect I wanted to consider was the consequences – both positive and negative – of going through the self-assessment process, and whether the trade-offs between them were too large to be worth it for clients (this is also called *consequential validity*). My questions here focused on how the tool bumped up against cultural norms and taboos, and what effect it had in terms of consciousness-raising and empowerment. I used focus-group discussions to explore topics such as collective empowerment, cultural norms and taboos, and conducted individual semi-structured interviews with clients and Loan Officers who had already completed the Poverty Stoplight visual survey to see if the Stoplight assessment had changed anything in their lives, and if it created any (negative or positive) results in the household. To my relief, clients, non-clients and Loan Officers across the board believed the Poverty Stoplight would have a positive effect in poor communities. Clients and Loan Officers, in particular, reported that the Poverty Stoplight helped clients see poverty in a different light—as a problem to be overcome rather than endured.

In terms of our ability to generalize the results (i.e. being able to draw conclusions from our data), I asked a few more questions about the color scheme, illustrations, whether misreporting was possible, the internal consistency of our poverty dimensions and the consistency of the distance between levels.

In general, all clients understood that red was worse than yellow, which was in turn worse than green. However, conceptually, the distances between these three options seemed to differ. For example, some respondents considered red to mean extreme poverty – people who 'don't even have bread to eat' – and green to mean 'rich' rather than 'non-poor'. In that case, yellow could be understood as a comfortable middle point. However, others understood red as poor, yellow as being on the way out of poverty and green as non-poor. In this context, yellow is still poverty, but not as much; and green is non-poverty, but not extreme wealth either. This problem is typical of ordinal scales: they help us understand which level is more or less than the others, but they are not good at determining the distance between the levels— in which case, this could be an important area of input from the Loan Officer when the head of the household takes the visual survey.

However, for the most part, Loan Officers reported that having three universally understood colors was simple and easy for the clients to understand; three colors was enough, and not too many, and allowed them to glance at a client's results and quickly assess their situation. Some also reported that the difference between red and yellow for some indicators was small, so it was difficult to know whether the client was red or yellow (another important point to put on my list of tweaks). Respondents also noted that the colors may come preloaded with assumptions and judgments. Potentially, families doing the Stoplight survey could be ashamed to admit being red in an indicator—and the questions may be leading when green is presented as the 'desirable option'. The same goes with illustrations, where people are smiling in the green definitions and frowning in the red ones.

Furthermore, my interviews revealed some cases of vague indicator definitions that needed to be addressed. For example, the vaccines indicator states that red is 'no family member is vaccinated', yellow is 'family members are partially vaccinated against major diseases: they are not vaccinated against all diseases or not every member of the family is vaccinated' and green is 'Family members are vaccinated against the most serious diseases and which are considered compulsory'. In this instance, it is unclear what is meant by 'the most serious diseases' and how many vaccines are necessary to be red, yellow or green.

I asked users to identify the most and least important indicators within each dimension, which provided an interesting insight into their priorities. In general, it was easier for all respondents to select important indicators than it was to select unimportant indicators, suggesting that few indicators could be considered superfluous. When asked which indicators were most important, clients, non-clients and Loan Officers all agreed: 'Safe Home', 'Problem- and Conflict-Solving Ability' and all the indicators related to income ('Income Above the Poverty Line', 'Stable Income' and 'Diversified Sources of Income'). When asked about the least important indicators, clients, non-clients and Loan Officers mostly responded: 'Sufficient and Appropriate Clothing', 'Influence in the Public Sector', 'Voting in Elections', 'Entertainment and Recreation' and 'Garbage Disposal'.

Most Loan Officers reported that, when guiding clients through the self-assessment visual survey, they had to translate the survey terms and definitions into words the clients could understand. Most of the time, this entailed translating to *Guaraní*, and sometimes simply using examples rather than reading the entire definition. Loan Officers reported that a big part of their job was to be patient and kind with their clients, explaining the concepts a few times until the client understood. Users flagged problems with definitions containing a word that clients did not understand, where clients interpreted a word in a narrower way than we had intended or where a term was distasteful to clients (such as the term 'sexual health').

Overall, I was satisfied that the research results confirmed the Poverty Stoplight was a valid tool, and highlighted areas for improvement. I acknowledge that some people are wary of the fact that the tool measures both concrete things (such as the state of a bathroom) and subjective things (such as self-esteem), and that it assumes self-reported data can serve as an approximation for both types. The criticism is not around the need to measure both the concrete and subjective, but that they need to be measured in different ways with different tools. Otherwise (according to Andy Carrizosa, one of my research assistants), it would be like using a thermometer to measure the temperature of water, and then trying to use that same thermometer to measure the volume of a radio. I don't want to say that these are invalid concerns, but at the same time, the beauty of the tool is in its simplicity—having everything in one place, making the invisible visible, and seeing the connections between the concrete and the subjective when it comes to quality of life.

Given that the primary objective of the tool is to unleash the trapped energy of poor families, to show them a picture of what's possible and to increase their self-efficacy, any concerns about the mixing of indicator types were, to my mind, outweighed by the need to represent family well-being in a holistic way—in all its subjective and objective glory. The Poverty Stoplight is, as it were, a radically different kind of thermometer.

HAVING FULLY EXPLORED the nature and extent of the limitations identified within the Poverty Stoplight, I must say I am fully prepared to accept them. I found that competing poverty-measurement tools commonly used by the microfinance industry are either completely objective (focusing on income poverty) or completely subjective (focusing on qualitative methods). Almost none of the tools combine qualitative and quantitative methods. No other tool is dual-use—meaning that ours is, to my knowledge, the only methodology that combines a poverty metric and a coaching process. Having both means we need to accept a few trade-offs, but to my mind, they are worth it.

After 18 focus-group discussions, 700 individual semi-structured interviews, 46 in-depth interviews with microfinance clients, a PWR exercise with 32 clients, and 650 applications of the Poverty Stoplight visual survey to a sample of 325 women across 24 locations in Paraguay, I was confident the Poverty Stoplight was fit for purpose. It is a tool that can empower poor clients, through self-diagnosis, to understand the intensity and characteristics of their own poverty. This, in turn, allows them to develop a customized family plan to address their most urgent concerns with mentoring and encouragement from staff. With a visual survey, and through a process of awareness raising and self-reporting, the Poverty Stoplight intends to generate information that is useful for both the household and the institution, as well as external stakeholders.

Admittedly, the Poverty Stoplight makes several controversial choices in its approach to measuring poverty. The biggest of these is that it prioritizes empowerment over extraction, which creates some measurement-based problems. While the poverty metric must, of course, be valid and reliable, its core focus is allowing poor families to properly understand and change their own reality—hence the tool's preference for actionable over representative indicators, and why it presents those actionable indicators as a dashboard rather than an index of one score.

When thinking about these criticisms, I keep coming back to the questions: Who is this information really for?

Who owns it? Policymakers might prefer aggregated statistics. Academics might prefer randomized control trials. But a poor family has no interest in the child-mortality percentages in a country. A poor family has no interest in the fact that participation in a microfinance program generally leads to an average increased annual consumption of 2016 PPP $13.48. Useful for policymakers and development organizations those facts might be, but they do nothing to help a poor family understand and overcome the unique constellation of deprivations in their lives, nor leverage the unique constellation of strengths they possess.

Of course, I understood the concerns I heard about the reliability, validity and utility of the Poverty Stoplight. But I wasn't prepared to correct for them without answering the fundamental questions of: Reliable for whom? Valid for whom? Useful for whom? Different stakeholders may have had different needs when it came to our design choices, but I was determined the Poverty Stoplight would be the first methodology to side with poor families themselves—it was, first and foremost, a metric designed for their own personal use. We wanted poverty elimination by the people and for the people.

That being said, just because we were clear about our aims didn't mean people were prepared to accept them. After exhaustive testing, I was satisfied that the Poverty Stoplight did what we wanted it to do. I was unprepared, however, for the skepticism, push-back and outright rejection I would receive from other organizations – both within Paraguay and beyond – when we took the Poverty Stoplight on the road.

CHAPTER 11
RESISTANCE

WHEN YOU DEEPLY BELIEVE in an idea, and that idea is met with equally deep resistance from others, it's difficult to avoid the sinking suspicion that you're the one to blame. That if only you were more articulate, respected, connected, persuasive, then people couldn't help but see that you are creating something of value to your community, and to the world at large. Truth be told, I've had my fair share of doors slammed in my face over the years (typical of most changemakers), by individuals and organizations that couldn't even imagine meeting me halfway in terms of how we thought about poverty.

In those moments, I find it's helpful to recall Ken Wilber's words on the question of perspective: "We're all climbing up the ladder of consciousness—and each person, rich or poor, has a personal perspective that is unique according to which wall their ladder is leaning against, and which rung of the latter they are standing on. We can understand the rungs below us that we've already climbed, but not the ones above us that we have yet to climb. Being on our own rung means that we are all rational in our own way—and that we can never understand someone else's perspective unless we can put ourselves on the same rung of the same ladder leaning against the same wall." When he said this to me, we were discussing the fact that helping our clients to see their deprivations is a necessary precondition for helping them to overcome them—but the same applies to my many failed attempts to convince other development organizations of the value of the Poverty Stoplight. As Wilber reminds us, "Sometimes people have to be assisted to climb their ladder of their awareness. You can't just plug your knowledge into their head, because it won't work in the way you expect it will."

For sure, I've climbed my own ladder over time. I honestly laugh when I recall the conversation with Luis Fernando, when he challenged me to define what I meant by the word 'poverty' (and how we were going to measure it) and the first idea I reached for was the national income-poverty line. At the time, I suspected that income wasn't the problem, but I only had anecdotal evidence to back up my claim.

Now, I had hard data. For example, in 2012, only 18 percent of our clients were income poor, whereas 34 percent were poor in nutrition, 27 percent lacked separate bedrooms and 25 percent were poor in personal and asset security. At the same time, only 6 percent had no cell phone, only 10 percent lacked proper clothing and only 10 percent had homes with unsafe roofs, windows and doors. So, income poverty is sometimes related to other types of poverty, and sometimes unrelated. Sometimes people are deprived because of a lack of money, and sometimes a lack of money is being driven by deprivations in other areas. After all, even a family with a decent income will suffer if they don't manage their money well.

What we've found is that the more difficult problems to tackle are the teeth, the booze, the violence—because the first step to doing so is to embrace the problem. In fact, the most frequent red indicators in the communities where we work are 'Personal Hygiene', 'Sexual Health', 'Capacity to Influence the Public Sector', 'Vaccines', 'Social Capital',

'Family Savings' and 'Elevated Stoves and Ventilated Kitchens'.

And this is precisely where the question of perspective becomes critical: it's not about whether we as an organization could see the problem—it's about whether the clients could see it for themselves. All those years ago, I argued with Luis Fernando about the lunacy of visiting a client's house, witnessing a family's many deprivations and not doing anything about them. He argued that it wasn't our job to solve all of those problems—and it took me years to figure out that he was right. It wasn't our job. It was theirs. But it was our job to help them see what was possible, to help them embrace two ideas: yes, fixing the problem was possible; and yes, it was worth it. And once they'd turned all their reds and yellows into greens, they'd be on their way: activated, motivated to tackle future challenges and on the path toward continually improving their lives and livelihoods.

While I appreciate that the Poverty Stoplight allows us, as a Foundation, to ask radically different questions about poverty and how to eliminate it, I've realized that other organizations aren't always prepared to listen to those questions when we articulate them.

AS EARLY AS 2011, we started meeting with UN Development Program (UNDP) officials in Paraguay, who were working with the Paraguayan Welfare Agency on a conditional cash-transfer program to promote the Poverty Stoplight as a potentially useful tool to support their work.

For those of you unfamiliar with conditional cash transfers, the basic logic is that the government cuts a welfare check that is contingent upon the beneficiary complying with a certain set of behavioral expectations (for example, sending their kids to school or taking them for regular doctor visits). An initial survey uses a handful of indicators to identify those who are poor enough to qualify as beneficiaries—and that data is also fed to the policymakers responsible for program development. Welfare is withdrawn if the family is seen to violate the conditions of the agreement (for example, if the kids start missing school or health visits) or if their living conditions improve.

From my perspective, the idea of a conditional cash transfer is missing the point. It's throwing money at a problem—and maybe not even the right problem, because it doesn't (and doesn't even try to) address the problems and deprivations that poor families experience.

The process begins with a long and complicated extractive paper survey called the *ficha* social, which uses more than 50 questions and dozens of sub-questions to decide whether a person is 'poor' enough to qualify as a beneficiary. On the face of things, it's encouraging that the *ficha* looks at a diverse set of quality of life indicators, not just income levels. However, the way the responses are weighted belies the government's belief that poverty is, by and large, a rural phenomenon. For example, one question considers the type of flooring material in the family's house: is it dirt, wood, brick, cement, tile, ceramic or carpet? As a result, an urban poor person (with a tile floor) is less likely to qualify than a rural poor person (with a dirt floor)—even if their monthly income levels are comparable and their lives are, in all other respects, very similar.

Worse, after the *ficha* has been completed, the Welfare Agency's thinking on multidimensional poverty (and concern for the well-being of the entire family) comes to an end. Once beneficiaries are approved for the program, they are provided with a small cash stipend to do well by their children by making sure they are vaccinated and attend school. The focus is on preventing the transmission of intergenerational poverty—meaning that the program does nothing to improve overall family well-being (to say nothing of income) in the here and now.

138

Not only that, but the program is designed to discourage families from improving their well-being once they have been accepted into it. Families qualify as eligible based on their deprivations in housing, health and other areas—and they know the cash bonus will be removed if they demonstrate improvement in any of them. In other words, the program creates 'poverty traps' that incentivize the parents to *not* improve their home, or to *not* invest in their business, or to *not* go to the doctor (despite sending their kids, as stipulated by the program rules).

Along the same lines, once rewards are withdrawn, there's a danger the 'positive behavior' they incentivized will stop— leading to poor parents potentially pulling their kids out of school because they built themselves a nice bathroom and got kicked out of the program. If this isn't a perfect example of a family held captive to someone else's definition of poverty, I don't know what is.

Finally, the government has no idea what 'success' looks like, other than expanding program outreach and increasing the number of people designated as 'poor'. That being the case, the government has no incentive to actually help people overcome poverty (much like the families it purports to help). To be sure, the program identifies the manifold deprivations the family has—but it does not share this information with the family, and it does nothing to help them overcome those challenges. So yes, the children are in school—but that doesn't mean the parents have enough money to feed them dinner when they get home. And yes, the children are vaccinated, but that doesn't mean the family has a roof that keeps the rain out.

Instead of paying people to stay in poverty, shouldn't we be helping them to get out of it? Shouldn't the government's anti-poverty policy be designed to provide families with the skills and motivation they need to earn above the poverty line and improve their quality of life? What if we had a program that paid people to *overcome* poverty? Think about it. The government could help families identify the things holding them back from being non-poor and cover the cost of sorting out those issues (new bathrooms, eyeglasses, etc.). With the Poverty Stoplight, it's possible.

At least, that's what I hoped to convince the Welfare Agency of. I wanted to show them how the Poverty Stoplight could help them take their work to the next level. I believed the Poverty Stoplight could help them create an anti-poverty policy that was effective and efficient, because it met the real needs of families and turned passive beneficiaries into active participants, so that everyone was working together toward a common goal.

The conversation didn't go well. The Welfare Agency Director began by assuring me their existing *ficha social* was perfectly adequate for their needs.

"Well, maybe it can be improved," I suggested. "Think of the advantages of having the head of the household become empowered through a process that gives the information she needs to tackle her own deprivations. After all, your program wants to bring families out of poverty, right?"

"To be honest, we are more concerned about the children than the mothers. We want to prevent intergenerational poverty," the UNDP representative informed me.

"But household poverty doesn't care whether you're an adult or a child. We need to get everyone working on the problem together. Yes, the kids need to be in school, but we need parents on board too, understanding and solving their challenges. We know they can juggle multiple issues, because they do it all the time. What's more, we've learned that no one family is poor in everything all the time. You're making the assumption that a family you identify as 'poor' in income is also 'poor' in education. What if that's not actually the case? How do you know that the thing these families need is an incentive to send the kids to school? What if you could tailor your program to what the family needed? It's true that the Poverty Stoplight contains more indicators than your survey, but by focusing on their poverty gaps, rather than their overall poverty, families find it easier to resolve specific problems one at a time."

"Do you mean income gaps?" the Welfare Agency Director asked. "We provide a small subsidy to families."

"A 'poverty gap' is what we call the distance between red and green – or yellow and green – in any given indicator. Let's take, for example, one of our poverty indicators: 'We earn income above the poverty line'. As you know, the Census Bureau and the National Planning Agency have determined that, in the metropolitan area, the poverty line is $3.50 per person per day. A family of four needs to make $14 per day to be considered 'not poor', which works out to be $420 per month. If that family is only making $300 per month, then their income gap is $120. When we break income poverty down in this way, overcoming it becomes a more manageable task. It's easier to design a strategy to motivate and train a family to earn an additional $120 in a month than to make change happen by simply telling the family that they are 'monetarily poor'."

"Our job is to motivate the mother to send her children to school, and we do that by providing cash payment. We don't think that we can teach a poor family how to earn $120 a month," said the Welfare Agency Director.

"That is the whole point that I am trying to get across. Our visual survey empowers mothers because they diagnose themselves and they get to keep the information for their own use. They own the information about the problem, and as a result, they own the solution. The conditional cash-transfer survey, on the other hand, is purely extractive. She never gets to see the information, she never gets to understand the results—the data is of no practical use to her."

"Yes, but what can the poor head of a household do with information about her poverty?" asked the UNDP representative.

"Well, for a start, she can design and develop her own poverty-elimination plan."

"What makes you think that's even possible? She can't even read or write!"

"It's straightforward social cognitive theory. People change when they can successfully answer two questions: 'Is it worth it?' and 'Can I do it?' These two questions represent the two principal elements of change: motivation and skills. The Poverty Stoplight demystifies poverty. It breaks poverty elimination down into small and achievable tasks, ones that are completely within their reach."

"That may be so, but how do you think that the Welfare Agency can benefit from your tool?" asked the Welfare Agency Director.

"The first end-user is the family itself, but the second end-user could be the Welfare Agency. First, it's useful for targeting: is this family poor or not? If so, how varied and intense are their deprivations? You could also use the information for monitoring how well your families do over time, and to coordinate with other agencies on specific services or design interventions to address different forms of poverty."

"So, the Welfare Agency would have all the family poverty plans?"

"The family would keep the family plans, but you can also easily convert the qualitative information you gather into poverty indexes and other quantitative data to facilitate impact analysis. For an organization such as yours, which works in the social services, providing evidence of sustainable impact is important."

Here, the Director of the Welfare Agency corrected me: "Of course, our main concern is impact. But we know we are having a tremendous impact. What we need is a bigger budget so that we can reach more people."

"Okay," I countered, "in that case, the best way to influence legislators to provide and expand your budget is to demonstrate your beneficiaries improve faster than similar families that don't get any subsidies. The Poverty Stoplight can do that, and it also will amplify your efforts because you'll activate the families to reduce their own poverty, rather than being passive recipients of welfare support."

There was a long pause. "I'm sorry," the Welfare Agency Director said. "We are more interested in preventing inter-generational poverty. We believe that due to early childhood malnutrition, this generation of poor mothers will never overcome poverty. In all honesty, many times we see our-selves helping the poor despite themselves."

"Are you telling me that you think the mothers you support are damaged merchandise?"

"I think that is a very strong phrase, but yes, they have been damaged by the system and by the structural forces that oppress the poor. Now Paraguay, like many govern-ments of the region, has opted to intervene with conditional cash transfers. We have evidence that most poor people are actually too malnourished to get out of poverty," said the UNDP representative, with an air of finality. With that, they got up to shake my hand.

I was dumbfounded. It was as if my meeting with the National Development Bank was happening all over again. Street vendors are the plague; poor mothers are damaged merchandise. They were never consulted about their own poverty, because they were seen as too poor and too hungry and too stupid to do anything about it. This had been my first real attempt to convince another development organiz-ation of the value of our work and, needless to say, I was disappointed about how the meeting concluded.

Still, that was nothing compared to the disappointment that awaited me when I tried to convince the entire Paraguayan government to adopt the Poverty Stoplight as its national poverty-elimination methodology of choice.

LESS THAN A YEAR LATER, all hell broke loose in a field in rural Paraguay. On a June morning in 2012, police arrived at the scene of a land grab underway in Curuguaty. Approximately 1,000 peasants had invaded a large plantation that had been occupied illegally by a rich landowner who had, at one time, been President of the Colorado Party. There was an ongoing land-reform program, and many peasants argued that they were each entitled to a 10-hectare slice of the plantation. They weren't going to wait for the government to give it to them—they decided to take it for themselves.

The Left-leaning government of the time, despite being sympathetic to the invading peasants, had accepted the Attorney General's position that the police should evacuate the premises. When police arrived, an ambush by armed peasants left six policemen dead. The police retaliated, killing 11 peasants and wounding many more. The situation quickly unraveled.

Our Mbaracayú agricultural school was located in the neighboring village, and a call from its Director revealed that students were frightened not only that their families might be caught up in the violence but also that it might spread. We also had many microfinance staff and clients in the area, and I feared for their safety. Not knowing what else to do, I hopped in the car and sped toward the Curuguaty branch office, toward the ugly face of rural poverty in Latin America: starving peasants rising up against the land-grabbing rich.

Thankfully, our local staff came through the crisis unscathed. As for the peasants, I had no doubt in my mind how this incident would end—until a conversation with a local Loan Officer revealed a startling piece of news: none of our microfinance clients in the area had been harmed in the land invasion. Why? Because none of them had taken part in it. They simply didn't bother. I pressed the Loan Officer for an explanation, and she shrugged her shoulders and smiled.

"It's simple," she said. "Our clients are all involved in overcoming poverty. They want to be green in everything. They are all busy with their microenterprises and they don't have time for things like land invasions. Many people here are subsistence farmers who believe the government owes them land and that owning land will mean they'll overcome poverty. But our clients know better. They know it takes more than money to be green in everything."

An idea was forming in my mind. As I returned to the city, I called my old friend (and then-Vice President) Federico Franco and told him what I saw. By the time we met face to face later that week, President Lugo had been impeached over the crisis, and Franco had accepted his constitutional duty to be sworn in as President and serve out the final 14 months of his term.

"I am very worried about the peasants of Curuguaty and their families," he admitted. "I'd like to ask you to collaborate with all the ministries and agencies that have social programs to develop a plan to help those poor people. Is that possible? And, if so, where should we start?"

"Well, first we need to listen to what the people themselves have to say," I said. "There are over 5,000 people in the area, living in five different villages. I have the poverty measurement tool just to do that. It's called the Poverty Stoplight. *Fundación Paraguaya* has been working in the area for many years and we know it well. I can prepare a plan and have it ready next week."

The Curuguaty Plan was launched on 23 August 2012. It was ambitious—because it needed to be. If you lived in Paraguay, you had a 35 percent chance of living in poverty. If you came from Curuguaty, that number jumped to 58 percent. Forty percent of people in Curuguaty were undocumented, 55 percent lacked access to drinking water, 15 percent were unvaccinated, 17 percent lived without electricity and 95 percent cooked with firewood. The recent uprising was a stark reminder that the time for half measures had passed.

So, based on national data and Poverty Stoplight data, we sought to identify and close the poverty gaps in the three key areas: land tenure, income and quality of life. So, for example, given that only 30 percent of local households had land titles, we'd support the remaining 70 percent to formalize their tenure. We'd assist the 1,450 poorest local families (out of 2,500 families in total) to earn the additional $150 per month they needed to rise above the poverty line. Finally, we'd use the Poverty Stoplight to help those 1,450 families self-diagnose their multidimensional needs, so that different government agencies and private companies could assist them or provide them with services. A detailed project-management system was devised to connect each objective with key tasks, as well as different government agencies and stakeholders with the specific deprivations identified by each family.

When it was launched, the plan generated a lot of complaints from the financial administrators of the various government departments, who hadn't anticipated being involved in this project when planning their budgets. As such, it was widely perceived as a burden rather than a unique opportunity. At least, *I* saw it as an opportunity. For the first time ever, the public and private sector would be able to come together around one single poverty-elimination project, and different public departments would be able to communicate and coordinate based on a shared language and set of objectives. What's more, no one would be going in blind; we would have detailed data on these families' demand for infrastructure, goods and services, and the families would report on their poverty in 50 indicators. Some of these deprivations called for government services, such as identity cards, vaccines, health posts and the like. Other needs were better resolved with private-sector solutions, such as owning refrigerators, access to credit and savings accounts. A detailed project-management system would hold it all together and hold us to our shared goals.

Better still, the local community also saw it as an opportunity, embracing it in a way I could never have hoped. Seven months later, more than 340 families had overcome extreme poverty in income, and 221 were generating income above the poverty line. In general, families increased their income by 36 percent. More than 436 families had started using a household budget, 393 had diversified their income stream, 541 had obtained loans and 314 had opened savings accounts. More than 150 families had improved their bathrooms, 234 had improved their nutrition, 221 had improved their personal hygiene and sexual health, 274 had their children vaccinated, 178 got hooked up to the electricity grid, 108 reported better home appliances and home furniture, 136 had improved their children's school attendance, and 475 heads of households participated in workshops and training courses related to self-esteem, autonomy, capacity to make decisions and entrepreneurship. In other words: in just seven months, 1,450 families made more than 4,000 improvements to their quality of life.

Even two months into the project, the results seemed so promising that I thought it was time to take our efforts to the national level. President Franco agreed, and invited me to a meeting with his cabinet and leaders from the private sector, including farming, ranching, manufacturing and services. Based on the conversations I'd had in advance with the key stakeholders, I was confident the room would be receptive to the national Poverty Stoplight plan (which we referred to as Apex)—especially those from the private sector, many of whom had confided that they were tired of being labeled 'insensitive' to the needs of the community.

"The Apex plan will require a big shift in how we work," I began. "First and foremost, our starting point will be what people actually need, and not the goods and services the government is currently offering. This is demand-driven poverty *elimination*, not supply-driven poverty alleviation or reduction. What's more, all the indicators are understandable and achievable by the families themselves. That allows us to monitor outcomes, not just outputs."

"Can you give us an example?" the Minister of Justice and Labor asked.

"Yes, of course. In the Curuguaty project, 176 families reported that they didn't know how to generate the additional income they needed to become green in 'Income'. So, we asked our colleagues at the National Professional Training Agency for help. They agreed, but then we realized all they did was offer training courses. They have no idea what happens to the family afterward; they only have a budget for training, they're only held accountable for delivering training sessions. As a consequence, they have no idea what their results are—whether families actually increase their income based on what they learn in the workshops. Seen from this perspective, they have no idea whether or not they're doing a good job, whether their training represents good value for money for the government. Unfortunately, most of our government services are only in the business of doing things, rather than understanding whether what they do actually makes a difference."

Here, the Minister of Finance chimed in: "Working with individual families and measuring results sounds expensive. Where is the money going to come from? And how much will this plan cost?"

"I can't tell you that," I said. "More to the point, no one can, until every extremely poor family in the country takes the survey. I know how much it costs to build a modern bathroom, but we don't know how many families need one. I know how much a new roof costs, but I don't know how many new roofs they will need. But I do know this: bringing someone from red in housing to green or yellow by improving what they already have will always be less expensive than building a new social-housing unit from scratch. That's why we shouldn't just be thinking about this in terms of cost, but rather in terms of *opportunity* cost. What will we save by fixing bathrooms and roofs rather than the government building new houses? What will we save by vaccinating rather than treating infectious diseases? No one knows. But we do know that the government and the private sector can work together to meet the demand identified.

"Just imagine how powerful this data could be," I continued. "For the private sector, it's like having someone do your market research for free. For the public sector, it's like being able to save money by not offering support where it's not needed. I know I'm asking everyone to take a big leap of faith on this project and work in a completely new way. But I also know it will be worth it. Both to you, and to the families."

"How many families are we talking about?" asked the Minister of Health.

"According to the last census, there are approximately 1.2 million people living in extreme income poverty in our country. With the Poverty Stoplight, that means working with 260,000 families, at a rate of 4.5 members per family."

"And how many government agencies will be involved?" the Minister of the Interior queried.

"All of them. We're counting on the full participation of all 11 ministries and 19 agencies, who will work alongside private-sector representatives for companies who will provide

149

employment opportunities and other services. But don't worry; not every ministry will be working on every indicator, and we've made a list so each agency is clear on which indicators it's involved in. We'll have regional and thematic coordination groups to keep project communication and coordination running smoothly, and a monitoring and evaluation unit to measure how fast extreme poverty is being reduced."

I wasn't surprised at the level of skepticism I met in the cabinet meeting. After all, I was asking them to completely reengineer the way they work in order to overcome bureaucratic inertia, inefficiency and senseless waste of resources. The Poverty Stoplight would have offered them a common language and a shared set of objectives. However, the voices of doubt started to overpower the voices of optimism.

The Census Bureau Director was the first to speak out. She doubted the validity of the survey technique, and only wanted to gather data that was internationally comparable. She pointed out that she had already collected income-poverty data, so why did we need to collect it again? Neither did she agree with the concept of a survey being used to raise awareness—and she certainly didn't hold with the idea of including subjective indicators, which would only 'contaminate' the data and make statistical inferences impossible.

The Census Bureau Director's complaint opened the door to other complaints. I was informed that most ministries and agencies were not used to working toward outcomes. Nobody wanted accountability for actual results. The only priority was to spend the agreed budget on approved activities—and the Poverty Stoplight was definitely not one of them. Furthermore, department heads thought it was unlikely that they could get their staff on board with the project. They had no budget for incentives, and couldn't fire staff members who didn't reach their targets.

In December, despite the concerns that had been raised, the President sent Apex to Congress, which declared the elimination of extreme poverty as a national priority for the next five years. The proposed law specified a human rights approach, a comprehensive and holistic focus on families as the unit of analysis, a focus on helping families achieve their own perceived potential, the co-responsibility of poor families and public-private partnerships to achieve goals, territorial targeting and geo-referencing, results-based evaluation, transparency and allowing families to self-diagnose their level of multidimensional poverty. It proposed a multisector coordinating council, tax incentives for the private sector and strict guidelines to prevent assigned budgetary resources from being diverted into non-extreme poverty endeavors.

By June, an open letter to Congress appeared in the newspaper, signed by the former President's head of social policy and other influential members of the current government. I quote:

> Extreme poverty has remained unchanged for over a decade, despite economic growth and the public policies implemented, denoting its structural character. This complex situation makes the attainment of the Apex's stated objective difficult, if not impossible, especially with a public sector lacking resources, weak institutions and no professionalized civil service. We are not aware of any international experiences that have succeeded, except for the 30 most developed countries of the world, where the tax burden is twice and thrice that of Paraguay.
>
> As well as eradicating extreme poverty, which is measured by income, the Plan seeks to affect other areas of life of the poor population that are

measured with indicators such as: self-esteem, moral consciousness, aesthetic self-expression, art and beauty, assertive behavior. These indicators have an important ethical connotation that cannot be defined in a Social Cabinet. Who defines what is moral and the subsequent moral conscience? A moral principle can be 'revealed' by God to a prophet, revealed in a mystical experience or constructed by reason. How will the Social Cabinet construct indicators of moral conscience or of assertive behavior or of aesthetic self-expression?

Given these considerations, eliminating extreme poverty and affecting the other aspects is an aspiration which shows a proposal lacking in seriousness or ignorance about Paraguayan reality, both in terms of its extreme poverty and its public management.

The facts that the main indicator of extreme poverty is income, and that the expected results are derived from access to employment, are evidence of the Plan's weakness, with the proposal of 'entrepreneurship' as one of its strategies. There is sufficient empirical evidence, in Paraguay and globally, that people cannot be lifted out of extreme poverty through small enterprises (mom and pop stores, handicrafts, small-scale agricultural production, all without quality standards). Without active financial inclusion, agricultural and labor policies, widespread coverage of the extremely poor population cannot be expected to generate stable and diversified income, to access credit and to save, as outlined in the Plan.

In addition to the above, the strategy of partnering with the private sector needs to consider several aspects. Living without extreme poverty is a right established in several international documents and in our Constitution. The eradication of extreme poverty is a public good due to its highly positive externality.

Therefore, poverty-reduction efforts cannot depend on the goodwill of the business sector or on its social responsibility, especially because in Paraguay low-productivity business sectors, such as micro and small enterprises; sectors evading the payment of taxes that fund public programs, i.e. the main instruments of poverty-reduction efforts; and sectors that do not comply with labor laws, when income and access to social security are also key factors to overcome poverty.

An obstacle to working with the private sector, whose fundamental principles are efficiency and profitability, is the scarcity of assets of adults living in extreme poverty: low human capital (health and education), small area of land and of poor quality, almost nil financial inclusion, and meager energy and road infrastructure in the districts where most of the extremely poor live. Plus, a broad heterogeneity of the families: some made up of older adults and children due to the migration of adults; others with women heads of household meaning women who require flexible occupations to combine paid work with family work. Given this scenario, one wonders how the private sector will contribute substantially to the elimination of extreme poverty.

The Plan seeks to target families living in extreme poverty. A targeting instrument should meet several requirements: be efficient in measuring what it is expected to measure, reducing errors of inclusion (incorporating a family that is not living in extreme poverty into the program) and of exclusion (leaving out those who should not be included), have a reasonable cost and allow assessment of the impact of the initiative after a prudent time of intervention. The latter two conditions are important, not only to evaluate the results, but also to provide transparency and accountability, basic principles of democracy.

The Apex proposes an instrument called the 'Stoplight', a qualitative tool that only seeks to capture the perception of how each family sees their own poverty. This approach has several flaws from the perspective of public management. First, it precludes a uniform criterion to define who is poor and who is not, which can generate problems of efficiency and transparency. Two families in similar situations might end up with one family living in extreme poverty and not the other one, since this condition will depend on the family's perception of their own poverty. As poverty reduction is highly beneficial to society, addressing the issue cannot depend on individual decisions. That is why primary education, vaccinations and the cleaning of vacant plots of land are compulsory, and non-compliance is penalized.

If we assume that extreme poverty has the same negative impact as illiteracy, a measles epidemic or the existence of breeding sites of *Aedes*

Aegypti mosquitoes, the decision of whether they are poor or not cannot be left to the discretion of the families. The state must be called to define whom to affect through its policy and must do so objectively.

Each public policy requires an impact assessment. In the rest of the world current and scientifically-proven impact assessment methodologies call for standardized indicators, which are not allowed in qualitative methodologies. The implementation of this instrument might be possible in small groups, but its operational and financial application to 200,000 families living in extreme poverty in Paraguay is highly unlikely.

Poverty-reduction efforts have a long track-record in Europe and Latin America, with successes and failures that have been studied and systematized by the academic community and international cooperation. Paraguay must use this accumulated expertise and create spaces for discussion, leveraging the efforts already in place to create a national research system and strengthen the role that universities should play in public policymaking, especially in the phases of design and evaluation.

Paraguay has also experienced advances that, with strengths and weaknesses, were first materialized in a National Poverty Reduction Strategy, and later in a Social Development Public Policy. Based on these guidelines, numerous social programs were created and strengthened that helped sustain a slow, but systematic, reduction of moderate poverty, alongside slow advances in other areas, such as in maternal and infant

mortality, access to safe water and social protection. All this based on international, especially
Latin American, experience. These programs
rely on selection and targeting mechanisms,
lessons learned, expertise, and recently, evaluations. No future anti-poverty initiative should
lose sight of the steps already taken.

The letter couldn't have been more comprehensive in its
condemnation of the Poverty Stoplight and our proposal to
implement it at a national level. It was also a stark reminder
of the many times I had listened to government bureaucrats
and economists, both from the Right and the Left, who perceived empowering the poor as a threat. Imagine the gall
of allowing poor people to define their poverty! What next?
Poor people leading government ministries?

By August, national elections had taken place, a new administration had taken office and the Apex plan was scrapped.
With the help of the World Bank, the new government created a traditional, top-down, unidimensional monetarist plan.
It shied away from the commitment to poverty elimination,
declaring 'poverty reduction' to be the national priority, and
tasked the National Planning Agency to draft the program
without input from the other ministries.

"There it is," I said to myself. "Goodbye poverty *elimination*, welcome back poverty *reduction*, whatever that means."
I still believed the Poverty Stoplight worked. I still believed
poor families weren't as apathetic and helpless as generally
believed. I still believed they could play the role of protagonist in the fight to eliminate their deprivations. But in that
moment, my belief in my ability to convince others that it
was possible, and worth it, was at an all-time low.

I OFTEN TRY TO IMAGINE what life would be like had
we never created the Poverty Stoplight. Back in the day, our

organizational goals were to increase client income, strengthen precarious jobs and create new jobs. We had all the data we needed to understand our 'impact'. I can confidently inform you that our clients tended to create 1.3 jobs per year. Some clients came to us earning only $36 per month; others as much as $360 per month. Some clients increased their income by 500 percent in a year, but the average was around 100 percent.

But so what? I can also tell you that sometimes it didn't work. Sometimes, clients were with us for 10 years or more and didn't increase their income at all—or they did increase their incomes, but they didn't experience the domino effects we assumed would automatically follow. Without detailed information about what was actually happening in the lives of our clients, it was natural to view poverty as one big black box. Poverty was something we didn't understand and couldn't possibly hope to move the needle on in any significant or systematic way. That's why, when I remember to heed Wilber's advice about perspective, I can understand the resistance we face from other civil society organizations that can't yet see the potential value that having detailed, family-level, multidimensional poverty data can add to their work. After all, the Foundation was standing on the same rung of the same ladder, once.

What I find harder to understand are people who somehow perceive the Poverty Stoplight as a threat. They simply refuse to engage in any conversation about poverty that could undermine their worldview. It's almost as if they know, deep down, that the emperor has no clothes—but no one wants to admit the truth for fear of appearing foolish. No one wants to admit that their work might not be as valuable as they'd always believed, because it would mean a lot of money and pride poured down the drain. No one wants to admit that they were too in love with their own solutions to stop and question their assumptions about who has the right to define the problem. No one wants more information about the problem if it implies the responsibility to act on it. Because when they assume that they own poverty, they *do* feel that responsibility. It's a burden, and maybe even a losing battle, but they do what they can—even when that means focusing their time and money on alleviating the symptoms of the problem, rather than tackling the problem itself.

Take, for example, my conversations with the Food Bank in Houston, Texas. In the typology of social-purpose organizations articulated by Sally Osberg and Roger Martin (in, among other places, their book *Getting Beyond Better*), the Houston Food Bank is involved in direct service provision to improve living standards within the existing equilibrium— plugging holes in an unjust system without trying to change that system. In other words, you go to them for a meal but not to tackle the underlying causes of the hunger problem in the city. In conversation with the Food Bank's Director, I learned they had distributed 122 million meals to 800,000 service users. For those who want to do the math, in their service area (covering 18 counties), that's 11 percent of the population. Over 1 in 10 people are poor in food and, on average, accept 3 meals a day for 51 days.

I was shocked at this statistic—but not as shocked as I was to hear that the Food Bank doesn't know why people are using it. They don't know what's causing the hunger problem; neither do they know whether they're dealing with chronic hunger or transitory hunger. To my mind, the Poverty Stoplight would help them understand what kind of poverty was bringing people to their door—and help them to do something about it. Was the problem that their service users didn't have enough income, or was there enough money but the boat was sinking because it had a hole where a family budget should be? Was a lack of health insurance in the face of long-term illness crowding out spending on food? Of course, no two people walking through their door would be grappling with the same constellation of challenges, but I had no doubt that those challenges were related to why they were using the Food Bank.

Yes, but that's not what we do. I hear this sentiment again and again, and not only from the Food Bank. I even heard it once from the mouth of from Luis Fernando, who, as you'll recall, didn't want the Foundation to get 'distracted' by anything other than income generation. Because the more responsibility we take on, the more overwhelming it can all become.

Here, too, I am reminded of a friend, the former mayor of Brasilia, who created the *Bolsa Familia*: Brazil's conditional cash-transfer program. On one occasion, when I told him how the Poverty Stoplight worked, he was incredulous. "You mean to tell me that the government will have to manage 30 million individualized poverty-elimination plans? That's too much work! It's physically impossible!" he exclaimed. He had missed the point that, thanks to technology, it would actually be 30 million heads of poor households creating and managing their own family plan. It wasn't his responsibility; it was the families' responsibility.

I know this because, time and again, we see families taking control of their lives in ways they never thought possible. They no longer rely on help to come to them. Interestingly, we've seen this create sizable shifts in community power dynamics. Traditional village leaders are being left behind. One of the traditional roles of a village leader is to take care of the needs of the community, in terms of acquiring and distributing resources, and to act as the formal intermediary between the village and the resource providers. However, without knowing precisely what those needs are, he (and it's usually a 'he') is reduced to leading by approximation. There was no way he could have known that in their village of 500 families, for instance, 129 families were red or yellow in 'School Supplies', 207 were red or yellow in 'Sexual Health' and 306 families were red or yellow in 'Appropriate Clothing'. And when the families saw the results of their visual survey, it wasn't the village leader they went to for help. They didn't need an intermediary; they went out and sourced their solutions themselves—from local companies, local government and local community groups. And sometimes, when they couldn't find the right solution, they created one of their own. This is possible because indicators place the responsibility squarely with the family and help the family become the protagonist of their own poverty-elimination narrative. *We save. We respect others. We are fully vaccinated.* We own our poverty, and we own the responsibility for becoming non-poor.

In the same vein, I've had the door slammed in my face by development organizations, which weren't interested in a methodology to support poor people to overcome their deprivations because their work didn't actually involve coming into direct contact with poor people. For instance, I recall one conversation with a representative from UNICEF Paraguay, who explained to me that UNICEF was "a rights-based organization, whose job was to research the well-being situation of mothers and children in the country and carry out advocacy activities at the policy level. We identify rights holders and duty bearers in relation to the Universal Declaration of Human Rights." In other words, it lobbies the government to increase the supply of social justice within the country, whereas the point of the Poverty Stoplight was to activate people's awareness of their rights and better articulate their demand for social justice from the relevant bodies—in this case, the government. If that's true, then shouldn't we be tackling the rights issue from both ends at once? After all, what good is an increased supply of rights if a population isn't activated enough to demand them?

More recently, as we've started to work with organizations in the US to apply the US version of the Poverty Stoplight there (including our partnership with Roots of Renewal in New Orleans—on which more later), I've heard a much more pernicious brand of resistance: the kind that rejects the validity of the Poverty Stoplight because it was developed somewhere else. "If it was designed in Paraguay, it can't possibly work here. Poverty in the United States of America is different." Is it, though? Each time we arrive in a new country, we go through the same community conversation process we went through to develop the Paraguay version—so the US version looks different than the Paraguayan version, which looks different than the UK version, all of which look different from the South African and Sierra Leonean and Singaporean and Papua New Guinean versions. The one shared feature of every country's Poverty Stoplight is this: it is defined by people in those countries with direct experience of the deprivations they describe and of what it means to be poor, very poor or not poor in each indicator.

Or maybe the resistance has much more to do with fear than we like to admit. Maybe the truth is that people simply don't want to know about the Poverty Stoplight because they are afraid of poverty; because poor people pose a threat to their comfortable lives. I recall once talking to leaders in the Paraguayan private sector and pitching them a kind of 'adopt a slum or rural village' idea. At the time, Paraguay had 1,500 poor slums and rural villages where extreme poverty was rampant. All these communities had thriving cattle ranches, soybean plantations or even urban manufacturing facilities nearby. To my way of thinking, all we needed were 1,500 business leaders willing to adopt one location and implement the Poverty Stoplight there.

The conversation didn't go well. Many of them could see the sense in what I was saying, but at the same time confessed their fear of visiting these cattle ranches or factories due to the risk of robbery or kidnapping. They were much more comfortable sticking with what they did best: producing wealth that would, in theory, trickle down to poor communities. After all, if wealth can trickle down, that means you never have to get up close and personal with poor people themselves.

Yet, despite all the external resistance we faced to the idea of the Poverty Stoplight, *within* the Foundation things appeared to be going well. Staff were quickly becoming more adept at applying the visual survey (the tablet version gave a big boost to the speed and appeal of the process), and clients loved the Stoplight, which turned everyone's ideas about poverty upside down—clients included. Time and again, we'd hear clients who had just completed their visual survey exclaim: "That's it? That's all poverty is? Easy—I can do that! I'm not as poor as I thought I was!"

Of course, that didn't mean that everything in the Foundation was smooth sailing. The truth was that I was soon in for a rude awakening—I just didn't know it yet.

CHAPTER 12
POVERTY-FREE CLIENTS…
AND STAFF

"WE ARE ALL POOR, MARTÍN." Those were Ken Wilber's parting words to me as I left his house in Colorado to begin the journey to Utah, where I would meet Joseph Grenny. Even those few hours spent in conversation with Ken left my mind in a spin, full of new ideas and new possibilities. It was as if I'd been dropped into a technicolor landscape after a life lived in monochrome. In short, it was a lot to process, so perhaps it's no wonder I didn't fully appreciate the significance of his last remark at the time. In fact, it took me years to finally understand, and I only did so after the staff revolt that Luis Fernando predicted came to fruition.

In any organization, there will always be some initial resistance to organizational change, no matter what that change is. It's not that Luis Fernando wasn't 100 percent committed to the mission of the Foundation, and it's not that he couldn't see the potential of the Poverty Stoplight to help us achieve that mission. However, it was also true that he had spent years turning the Foundation into a well-oiled machine that achieved the improbable: reaching institutional financial self-sufficiency, by providing tiny loans to high-risk clients, through a team that handled large client portfolios with a high level of operational autonomy across a huge geographical area. There were a lot of moving parts to our business, and he'd spent years tinkering until he'd gotten it just right. It was only natural that he didn't want anything to undermine that result.

Acknowledging his concerns, we agreed on what I thought was a conservative rollout plan of the Poverty Stoplight between 2011 and 2013. Loan Officers would handpick 10 percent of their clients to take part in the pilot—the ones they felt might be the easiest to work with (in other words, the 'low-hanging fruit'). In all, our 55 Loan Officers mentored an average of 105 families each, amounting to 5,775 families (out of our total portfolio of 57,585 at that time). Loan Officers would be responsible for helping all these families to get to green in income, and helping half of them get to green in all 50 indicators. This felt like a reasonable means of 'learning by doing'—and doing a little good along the way.

In 2012, our microfinance clients had an average of eight yellows and one red. Their most common deprivations were 'Capacity to Plan and Budget', 'Garbage Disposal', 'Income above the Poverty Line', 'Proper Roads', 'Savings', 'Healthy Teeth and Eyesight' and 'Separate Bedrooms for Adults and Children'.

To my relief, clients loved the Poverty Stoplight. Again and again, they'd point to it as proof that the Foundation really cared about them as families, not just as clients. That accolade quickly turned into hard numbers in the form of lower client drop-out rates, lower loan-default rates and higher client satisfaction results—three crucial data points to reassure Loan Officers they were on the right track. Meanwhile, with repeated practice in applying the visual survey and mentoring methodology with clients, Loan Officers found that the Poverty Stoplight wasn't such a burden after all. You could tell this by the way they described their task: not as a responsibility to lift a family out of poverty, but as a chance to help the family seize opportunities and leverage tools they already had in order to improve their lives. It wasn't an evaluation; it was a *self*-evaluation. It wasn't doing problem-solving for clients; it was a mentoring tool to match clients' needs with proven solutions.

To that end, our 'solutions bank' was quickly filling up as staff started sharing their ideas and brainstorming challenges with each other. Sometimes these conversations were about connecting clients with existing solutions; for example, one Loan Officer discovered that a local dentistry school offered free services on the weekends as a way of providing hands-on practice to their students and community outreach at the same time.

Other times, our staff used their own initiative to create new solutions—which is how, for example, our 'Clients Club' program came about. Faced with a number of clients who all needed to install modern bathrooms, one of our Loan Officers approached a local building-supply store to negotiate a group discount on new toilets. The agreement was that the Loan Officer would drive all of her clients' business to the store in exchange for the store offering them a 10 percent discount on materials. From there, the Clients Club Card idea snowballed; we eventually had 400 suppliers participating in the program, offering everything from bricks to toilet paper, from free gym passes to discounted movie tickets, from adult education to life insurance.

What's more, when we realized that many of our clients did not have access to health insurance – particularly in the countryside – we created our own through the Clients Club program. We partnered with 27 private hospitals and clinics, which offered our clients low-cost access to an annual medical check and up to five routine diagnostic tests per year (blood and urine, x-ray, pap smear, dengue fever, influenza, etc.). We also partnered with dental clinics and labs to offer similar discounts to not only our clients as individuals but also their entire family.

We also expanded membership of our Clients Club to non-clients. By 2017, over 85,000 new families had enrolled, paying an annual membership fee of $25 (compared to the $14 fee for clients). Collecting membership fees for the Club Card served two purposes: First, it underscored the point that it's not charity; second, our bylaws stipulate that all *Fundación Paraguaya* programs must be financially sustainable. At the time of writing, our Clients Club currently produces $200,000 per year for the Foundation – one-fifth of our annual microfinance program surplus – while providing important savings and benefits to our clients.

I have my staff to thank for the idea of systematically documenting all proven solutions to each indicator, which serves as a kind of ever-evolving knowledge bank for Loan Officers to draw on as they mentor clients. For insisting that all the solutions included in the solutions bank are sustainable, I have Luis Fernando to thank. We are a self-sufficient business helping our clients to become self-sufficient. We are not a charity, and our clients don't need gifts. What they *do* need is a bit of a break. For that reason, we're not going to buy wheelchairs in bulk and distribute them free of charge to clients in need—if we did, we'd eventually run out of money without having solved the underlying problem. This is a key distinction, and one that has been a guiding principle from the outset.

Making the Poverty Stoplight financially sustainable meant making it an efficient process. Staff found that the more they applied the paper-based survey, the better they got at doing it, and the less time it took. Usually, they could complete a survey in a little over an hour. But I knew we could improve on that, and that a technology platform was the key. Halfway through our two-year pilot with the visual survey, we introduced the new tablet system we had developed with HP. Here, too, Luis Fernando insisted on a cautious approach. We put the tablet technology into the hands of 12 Loan Officers in 7 of our branch offices, to be used with 480 clients in total (less than 10 percent of our 'low-hanging fruit' clients). Perhaps in this instance, however, our caution wasn't justified. Clients loved the new technology, seeing it as an exciting and fun addition to the process. Staff also embraced it, because it helped them to cut the time needed to do the visual self-assessment survey by two-thirds.

So, while I faced external resistance from the government, the UNDP and other development organizations about the validity and utility of the Poverty Stoplight, all signs within the Foundation pointed to staff and clients positively embracing it. At least, that's what I thought was happening.

That's when Luis Fernando cornered me with unsettling news. The truth was: the more clients our Loan Officers helped to overcome poverty, the less satisfied those Loan Officers were. Luis Fernando didn't mince his words: "Honestly, Martín, some of our Loan Officers are really upset by this. They feel that we worry too much about our clients and not enough about our own employees. What they really want is to participate in the Poverty Stoplight program themselves."

This news left me speechless. We had designed the Poverty Stoplight to help our poor clients lift themselves out of poverty. How could my own staff be so poor that they wanted to use it too? *It didn't make any sense.*

IN OUR EARLY DAYS as an organization, we were more or less flying blind when it came to human resource (HR) management policy and practice. There was no tradition or canon of HR 'best practice' in Paraguay that we could draw on; we were operating in a highly planned economy, dominated by a small handful of large corporations (mostly foreign-owned), in an ocean of small- and medium-sized businesses. Even today, small businesses dominate our economy: a working Paraguayan has a 95 percent chance of having fewer than 50 colleagues.

The lack of a national pool of talented HR Managers might stem from the fact that attracting and retaining the best talent wasn't really something that most companies worried about. Most workers at the time had a job for life rather than a career trajectory. Job stability trumped job satisfaction, especially for a low-wage, low-skilled worker who lacked the qualifications to find a better position elsewhere. There's also a law in Paraguay (on the statute books even today) that, after ten years in a job, a worker can't be fired—so apart from ensuring that working conditions are reasonably safe, there's little incentive for a company to invest in staff satisfaction.

Short of any real guidance on what I should be doing, I followed a rather more 'gut instinct' approach to HR development at the Foundation. I decided that our initial hiring criteria would simply be to find people who were willing to collaborate in teams and learn new things. We looked for positive attitudes rather than hard skills, figuring that the latter would be far easier to teach than the former. I also decided I wanted to create 'jobs for life' based not on personal apathy or legislative restrictions, but by creating jobs our staff *wanted* to keep for life—and were proud of for life.

For that to happen, we decided we had to pay our staff competitive salaries and create an environment where staff felt valued and respected. Yes, our staff have decent pensions and good health insurance, but they also benefit from continuous training and a significant voice within the organizational decision-making process. What's more, they feel part of something important, and connected to our organizational mission. This isn't just wishful thinking; if you walked into any Foundation office anywhere in the country and talked to any member of staff, you'd hear them confidently tell you about the Foundation's vision, mission and objectives. They might have applied for a job because we are well-respected for *what we do,* but they stay because of *how we do it.* This is because each person in the organization – from senior management to the janitors and everyone in between – 'walks the talk' of poverty elimination in Paraguay. That's why they stay. And they do stay. In 1985, we had 20 members of staff. In 2018, we had almost 500—and, of those original 20, five were still with the Foundation (including me).

I'm not telling you this to make myself seems like some brilliant and visionary organizational leader, because I'm not. I take too long to learn lessons, I fail to heed good advice and I let idealism cloud my better judgment more often than I care to admit. Also, apart from making a few key hiring decisions in the early days, I was never actually in charge of HR. That particular task fell to one Rodrigo Alonso, who joined the Foundation early on and worked his way up to be our first (and only) Head of HR. Today, he knows our procedures and policies inside out and takes the lead on staff recruitment, hiring, training and placement. That *Fundación Paraguaya* is a great place to work is a testament to his commitment and leadership, truly. We are lucky to have him. (And it was to him I turned, early on in the Poverty Stoplight development process, to help me make sense of the mountain of indicators I'd compiled.)

Under Rodrigo's guiding hand, we made the Foundation a great place to work. That's why I had a hard time comprehending Luis Fernando's news. What did he mean when he said staff were demanding to be able to apply the Poverty Stoplight to themselves? Did that mean some of our staff were poor, despite all the effort and attention we'd poured into creating a positive work environment? That they were poor despite earning a competitive wage and having great benefits? While we knew some of our staff came from humble origins, by and large our team is made up of middle-class Paraguayans with a university degree in law or accounting or business. While I found this news baffling, I didn't hesitate for a moment about what to do with it.

Rodrigo, on the other hand, didn't take kindly to my decision. I asked him to hand off all his regular duties to a deputy and, instead, to focus exclusively on guiding each and every member of our staff through the Poverty Stoplight process. His initial reaction was that he was being demoted. He couldn't understand why his portfolio was being taken away from him, or why he was being tasked with what he viewed as a 'pet project' with clients.

I can't blame him. None of us really understood the depth of the challenge I had laid at his door because no one had ever done it before—no one had ever climbed that ladder against that wall. And, once we got started, it was clear that nothing would ever be the same again.

APPLYING THE VISUAL SURVEY with staff was the easy part. Believing the survey results? That was the difficult part. We were shocked at how many staff members turned up yellow and red in income: 18 people on our payroll (out of 100 at the time) were living in income poverty or extreme income poverty. This wasn't because their salary was low in absolute terms but because it was low relative to the number of mouths they had to feed. What's more, our staff suffered an average of 5 yellows and 2.4 reds—in other words, more average reds than clients (who averaged 1 red per family).

And yet, perhaps, that's what Ken Wilber meant when he said we are all poor. All this time, we had been applying the Poverty Stoplight to our clients: clients who we approached because they looked like they might tick the income-poverty box; clients who, once they'd taken the Poverty Stoplight survey, might or might not have been red or yellow in income but were certainly grappling with deprivations in other areas of their lives. Whereas our staff, in theory, should have been green in income, and – according to the logic of the World Bank and the entire microfinance industry – green in everything else as a result. If we were looking for the final nail in the coffin of 'fix income poverty and the rest will fix itself', this was it.

The staff survey results also made us question the value of our client education programs. Knowledge is power, or so the theory goes. Our Loan Officers ran training modules on basic concepts in business and financial management as part of their group meetings. Because of this, we were certain they knew the value of savings and of having a family budget—they taught these skills to clients every day. Yet the survey revealed the startling truth: Of our 55 Loan Officers, 49 percent were red or yellow in 'Savings', and 46 percent were red or yellow in 'Family Budget'.

It turns out *knowing* is not enough; *doing* is what matters. For development organizations, training people isn't enough because *outputs* aren't what matter; *outcomes* are. I had argued this very point in my conversations with the UNDP and the Welfare Agency over conditional cash transfers, but here was proof that I had yet to learn the very same lesson.

Ken Wilber was right: We were all poor. We didn't save. We didn't budget. We didn't have modern bathrooms. We didn't have families free from violence. We all slept in the same bed. We should have known better, but we didn't. Non-poor families are all alike; every poor family is poor in its own way.

We had work to do.

WHILE THE POVERTY STOPLIGHT allowed our clients to own the poverty they had always experienced, it also allowed our staff to experience the poverty they had never owned up to.

Wilber opened our eyes to the challenge, and Grenny helped us to tackle it. Here's why: knowing wasn't the problem. It wasn't about inserting more knowledge into the heads of our staff, like they were some vessel waiting to be filled, as Paulo Freire pointed out. It was about changing behavior and helping our staff to do things they'd rather not do. Given the choice, I'd much rather read a book than run a marathon, and I'd much rather butter my bread than worry about my cholesterol.

Interestingly, guiding a concentrated community (our staff) through the Poverty Stoplight process allowed us to create solutions that activated social sources of influences. Until that moment, we'd been mentoring each client on a one-on-one basis, and that client might have been the only person in her community to be doing the Stoplight. We could activate sources of influence at the *personal* level—by motivating and helping clients to practice new skills. We could activate sources of influence at the *structural* level—for example, through programs like the Clients Club Card, which changed the economy of positive behavior change. But, unless a client knew another family that also happened to be going through the Poverty Stoplight process, we had no opportunity to activate *social* sources of influence—in other words, peer pressure and peer support.

All that changed when we applied the Stoplight to staff—a concentrated group of individuals all working toward the same goal (in their own ways). Becoming green in everything was the goal—and to help them love to do what they hated, we had to make it fun. That is why we turned to gamification to transform poverty elimination into a competitive sport. We knew gamification worked; we were using it to help teenagers become budding entrepreneurs through our youth-entrepreneurship programs.

The first poverty-elimination competition we ran with our staff was called 'I Look Good, I Feel Good'—and we're still running it to this day. In the latest round, staff from 24 of our offices organized into 22 teams of 10 to support each other to improve their health by losing weight (for those who wanted to get green in their 'We Like Our Appearance' indicator). Results were based on the difference between the weight of the entire team at the start and finish of the four-month competition. The buzz around the office for these events is always incredible—and this year was no exception. Everyone really got into the spirit of the competition and came up with innovative ways of tracking progress and encouraging each other. Some teams took advantage of the Club Card discount at the local gym to join a Zumba class together. Luis Fernando was the leader of his team, which created a dedicated WhatsApp group to report the results of their daily weigh-ins and share photos of each and every meal they ate (to prove they were following a healthy diet). By the end of the competition, Foundation staff were collectively 253 pounds lighter, and the winning team (of nine people) had lost a total of 88 pounds. As their reward, they each received a $50 deposit in their individual savings accounts from the Foundation.

Two years ago, we launched an annual 'Get Green' competition, in which branches and departments form teams to compete to win the most points (and a nice cash prize). Points are awarded on a sliding scale for every indicator: 10 points if every team member (who starts as red or yellow on that indicator) gets to green; 5 points if some, but not all, team members get to green (from red or yellow) on that indicator and 0 points if no team member gets to green. To secure their points, the team presents before-and-after photographic evidence (in the case of physical things, like home improvements) or photocopied documents (in the case of things like new savings accounts, new insurance policies or updated eyeglass prescriptions) for each indicator.

Another means of creating peer support and encouragement was to launch our 'heroes' bulletin. Each week, we celebrate one of our staff members overcoming one of their deprivations. Each bulletin gives a 'before and after' snapshot of the situation, with reference to the particular indicator, and provides an uplifting story of change. The underlying message is: deprivations are nothing to be ashamed of. Instead, we created a permanent and visible reminder that we all face challenges—and that, with the right support and encouragement, we can successfully face them.

Our growing enthusiasm for gamification led us to start competitions for clients. In 2015, we started running client poverty-elimination campaigns, using social media to create buzz around each one. For example, the 'My Bathroom, My Kitchen, My Pride' competition gives a cash prize of $530 to the winning client in each category, as well as $1,800 to the village banking group whose member wins the competition (thus creating peer support for individual achievement). Clients submit 'before and after' photos of either their bathroom or kitchen, and a staff jury chooses 24 finalists to compete for public votes in an online survey via Facebook. In 2017, for example, participants oversaw the construction of 752 new bathrooms and kitchens. Of these, 259 were finished in time to be considered in the selection of competition finalists, and 11,395 people participated in the public vote. We ran a similar competition, called 'My Happy Smile', in which clients competed for 'most improved smile' after fixing their teeth.

The beauty of these types of events is that we, as a Foundation, can influence massive amounts of positive change for very little investment. For instance, in the case of the bathrooms and kitchen competition, our financial outlay was $4,660: $530 each for the two winners in two categories (bathroom and kitchen) and $1,800 for each of their village banks. With 752 new kitchens and bathrooms being built, our per-unit investment was about $6 each—not to mention the incalculable 'nudging' value of getting over 11,000 people involved in a virtual conversation about the importance of having a modern bathroom or kitchen.

We also ran a five-month challenge competition, called 'Poverty Olympics', in which 4,300 teenagers competed to get their families out of poverty in selected indicators, such as 'Family Budget', 'Savings', 'Bathroom' and 'Diversified Sources of Income'. If you don't believe me when I say it's possible to unleash massive amounts of latent energy and resources within a family, let me say this: there is no force for social change more potent, more formidable, than a teenage girl competing for a free week-long holiday on a Brazilian beach. She will lobby her parents to open a savings account, to buy insurance and to use a family budget; she will gladly volunteer her time to teach financial literacy at a nearby school; she will write a song about poverty, if she wants to. After all, the dream of taking a 24-hour bus trip to the far-away Atlantic Ocean is too thrilling to pass up. And for us as a Foundation, being able to focus all that adolescent energy on tackling poverty is simply thrilling. In 2018, for example, 649 teams from 121 schools in 41 cities participated in our Poverty Olympics.

From the participants' perspective, these are fun and engaging ways to tackle their deprivations. From the Foundation's perspective, they are a great way of building buzz and getting big results for very little investment. Our role is limited to activating all six sources of influence, as suggested by Grenny: helping individuals to believe in themselves and master new skills, creating group accountability and support for individual change, and providing structural incentives and support for positive behavior change.

By being smart influencers, in 2017 we not only influenced 752 families to build bathrooms and kitchens but also influenced 96 people to get their teeth fixed, 360 families to work together on local environmental clean-ups, 465 clients to lose weight, 698 women to encourage their friends to go to their local clinic for pap smears and 204 new client self-help groups to form. We also saw 1,080 people participate in our 'Singing Entrepreneurs' competition, 100 people participate in our 'I Know Local News' competition, 480 in our sports competition, 204 in our 'My Neighbors Take Care of Me' competition and 720 in our 'Green in Everything' competition. This last one, in particular, was our first effort to enable families to overcome poverty without external mentoring or assistance. This is significant because it frees up staff time and allows us to experiment with gamification strategies that can run on their own, with minimum nudging and influencing from us.

What's more, helping our staff to eliminate poverty proved excellent preparation for the next phase in our journey to mainstream the Poverty Stoplight: creating Business Without Poverty, in Paraguay and beyond.

Martha Raquel Zayas: "My bathroom, my pride"
before and after

Mirian Raquel Vera: "My happy smile" before and after

CHAPTER 13
POVERTY-FREE BUSINESSES

IT ALL GOES BACK TO the question of numbers. The challenge of global poverty is huge, and in comparison, the Foundation is tiny. We believe the Poverty Stoplight is an effective methodology to measure and eliminate multi-dimensional poverty. But believing it isn't enough. If it's truly going to make a dent in a global-sized problem, we need more people to start using it.

By 2013, we'd had some successes bringing on Poverty Stoplight partners around the world. Some of these partner-ships were with organizations similar to *Fundación Paraguaya* that wanted to use the Poverty Stoplight with their own clients and beneficiaries. Each time we took the Stoplight to a new country, we went through a process (similar to the one I had done with our clients) to localize the indicators, the thresholds between indicators and the visuals that formed the backbone of the survey.

At the time of writing, more than 250 organizations are using the Poverty Stoplight, either through our 12 hubs in Argentina, Chile, Colombia, Honduras, Mexico, Nigeria, Papua New Guinea, Sierra Leone, Singapore, South Africa, the UK and the US, or through special projects we have (or have had) in Bolivia, Brazil, Burundi, China, Costa Rica,

Dominican Republic, Ecuador, Guatemala, India, Indonesia, El Salvador, Kenya, Nicaragua, Pakistan, Peru, Philippines, Puerto Rico, Senegal, Taiwan, Tanzania and Uganda.

On the other hand, as I've mentioned, we also had our fair share of doors slammed in our face by those who didn't see the value of the Poverty Stoplight—including various UN agencies and our own government. Yet, interestingly, one of those doors didn't stay closed for long. We were about to make the private sector an ally in our poverty-elimination work.

One day, I received a phone call from a former intern, Eduardo Gustale, who (after graduating from university in Chile) had landed a job as the Head of Corporate Social Responsibility at the Paraguayan Association of Christian Entrepreneurs (or ADEC, its Spanish acronym). He saw an opportunity to offer the Poverty Stoplight as a service to ADEC members and wanted to sound out my level of interest.

I didn't hesitate for a moment: it was a *yes*. Why? Because, having applied the Poverty Stoplight with Foundation staff, it was clear to me that we needed to take this to every single business in Paraguay. The private sector is a powerful force in the world—what if we could harness it as a force for good? Collaboration with ADEC (and 24 of its member businesses) would be the perfect opportunity to test that idea and develop the strategies and systems we needed to make it successful.

Quite rightly, Luis Fernando reminded me that, if we were to pursue this new opportunity, it must be designed to be sustainable. We were a financially self-sufficient organization and not in the business of subsidizing private companies, no matter how noble their aims with regards to staff well-being. We settled on a package of support services that included training the company's HR department to guide its staff through the visual self-assessment survey, supporting them to mentor their employees and making our bank of solutions available to them. The company does the rest themselves, and they commit to sharing what they're learning with us and each other.

Interestingly, it was the same business leaders who had rejected my idea of eliminating poverty in the slums near their factories who were receptive to the idea of becoming 'businesses without poverty'. The irony of refusing to help the nearby village or slum but agreeing to help their own people – many of whom probably lived in that same slum – didn't pass me by.

Seen from a certain perspective, this also perfectly illustrates the natural limits of Corporate Social Responsibility (CSR). CSR programs convert profit-maximizing businesses into good corporate citizens that run ethical programs for their staff, their community and the local environment. For example, a CSR initiative might mean building a football field for kids in the local community, sponsoring a community litter-picking event in a nearby park or offering free gym membership to company employees.

But from my perspective, CSR suffers from the same lack of clarity as traditional poverty-reduction efforts. That is to say: How much CSR is enough CSR? How do we know we're doing the right CSR? What actually happens as a result of our CSR, and does it even matter? Do we actually need to prove that it works? Is simply doing CSR enough? Can we just assume that, if we do CSR, the community, the environment and our employees will automatically benefit?

Most importantly: what benefits do the companies themselves derive from CSR? When I first pitched my 'adopt a slum' idea to local business leaders in 2012, they flatly rejected it. Their stated reason was that they were too afraid to enter the slums—but what if it wasn't fear after all? What if they simply couldn't see the point of doing so? Perhaps they felt that intervening in the poverty landscape of the community surrounding their factories wouldn't have delivered any direct benefits to the company itself. Yes, a company involved in charitable activities might be seen to be 'doing good' in the community—and perhaps, in the short term, by increasing its reputation capital the company could create new customers and increase the loyalty of existing ones. Conversely, in the long term, a company will only undermine its potential future profitability by destroying the community and environment in which it operates. But both the actual impact of CSR and the counterfactual of *not* doing CSR are difficult to define and prove.

Perhaps for that reason, the concept of CSR is subject to intense debate. Without being able to define it, without being able to measure the impact of it, without knowing who benefits more (the company itself, or the community, environment and employees?), who can say whether CSR is a valuable approach or simply an elaborate 'smoke and mirrors' exercise?

In contrast, the Poverty Stoplight offers companies a concrete and finite goal: for all employees to become green in everything. It's not about arbitrary ethical initiatives for employees that look good on paper but deliver unknowable value to the company and beneficiaries. By all means, offer a staff discount on gym memberships and call it CSR. Healthy employees are happy employees, right? But how do you know that's what they really need? How do you know there isn't something they need more? How can you assume that every employee has the same needs? On the other hand, the Poverty Stoplight generates detailed information on the extent and depth of deprivations facing each employee, so that the company can respond with the right programs for the right people. The Poverty Stoplight isn't charity—it's a productivity tool that companies can use to target the things that keep their employees from being the best they can be on the job.

For example, one of our corporate partners reported that his company was saving money by using the Poverty Stoplight because it helps personnel retention, increases motivation, reduces absenteeism and makes workers feel that the company cares about them—among other things. Instead of community development, it's employee development. You might think this is a bold claim, but I believe the Poverty Stoplight has the potential to change the face of CSR forever by helping companies identify areas of greatest need and avoid spending money (and reputational capital) on superfluous projects.

After all, what's the point of running charity projects in the local community when it's your employees who are living in extreme poverty? What's the point of offering programs for staff that don't address their actual needs? When a company has the data it needs to make the right decision about precisely how to be a good corporate citizen, that's unbelievably powerful. And sometimes that data acts as a powerful wake-up call.

I can't count the number of times a company we work with was left speechless at the results of its initial staff survey. Imagine a big supermarket chain finding out for the first time that one in five employees is poor or extremely poor in food. Imagine that company's shame that their staff are poor in the very thing the company sells.

Or, imagine a bank finding out that of its 30 employees, only 4 have saving accounts, only 8 have a stable income, only 16 have access to credit and only 19 have more than one source of family income. Or, imagine when a company paying the national minimum wage learns that a significant number of its employees are living in extreme income poverty. Or, imagine a company that offers a decent health and pension package but its workers report on their visual survey that they don't have insurance. How can that be?

What's the gap between having insurance and knowing that you have insurance? Is it because employees are too lazy to read the information packet they received when they joined, or is it because the company didn't bother to explain it to them in the first place? Without the Poverty Stoplight, would that company ever have known that there was a potentially huge health problem bubbling away just under the surface? What would happen if one of those staff members became seriously ill but didn't seek medical support because they didn't know they had insurance? Apart from anything else, what would happen to their on-the-job performance?

Yes, these are all disturbing results—but they also show the power of having family-level data rather than aggregate percentages. If you told an HR department that 20 percent of its staff disposed of their garbage by burning it in their backyard, what could they really do with that information? They could offer an environmental stewardship awareness course to all of their staff (wasting the time of the other 80 percent of staff who don't burn their garbage). They could put up an informational poster on recycling in the staff break room in the hope that the message gets through to the right people and that they act on it.

On the other hand, if that HR department knew the names of staff who didn't score green in the 'Garbage Disposal' indicator, or whose families all sleep in the same bed, or who don't have running water—they can approach them all, individually or as a group, and find out what it would take to get everyone to green in that indicator. Could the company provide a loan to build additional bedrooms, or a competition to encourage staff to 'throw away bad garbage habits', or invite a member from the local water company to the factory to sign up staff members for service?

Imagine this kind of targeted and direct problem-solving and solution-finding within companies. Now imagine if every company did this as part of 'best practice' HR management. We could put not only CSR to employees in a museum but also CSR to communities—because every family within that community will have someone working on their Poverty Stoplight through their place of work.

While we're at it, if every multinational company in the world used the Poverty Stoplight with its entire value chain, we might need to build a separate museum display case for the fair trade movement. Hear me out: Fair prices for producers are obviously important. Banana producers can be paid well for their products, but that doesn't mean their troubles are over. We know now that being green in income is only the start. What about the family budget? What about the family savings? Are all the kids in school? Is the house safe? With the Poverty Stoplight, companies could help suppliers eliminate their multidimensional poverty, not just earn a fair price.

In fact, in conversations with some of the leaders of the movement, it's been admitted to me that the idea of fair trade is running out of steam. Why? Because people want to know what impact it's having on the families. Like the microfinance industry, the fair trade movement is promoting increased income as an effective and automatic link to broader well-being gains—that paying a bit more for bananas means the kids are in school, the babies are healthy, the women empowered and the community stronger. But is it really working? Experience suggests not. Xavier Lazo (Ecuador's Minister of Agriculture and former banana exporter) told me how he witnessed many banana growers who, despite benefiting from fair trade prices, were still languishing in rural poverty (more on this later). Given all the Foundation has learned by using the Poverty Stoplight, this doesn't surprise me.

While acknowledging the gap between good intentions and desired results, when we consider the tools and frameworks available when the fair trade movement began its work, I think it did the best it could in terms of articulating the theory of change that underpins its work. What I'm saying is that now, we have the opportunity to do better—either by using the Poverty Stoplight to strengthen fair trade programs or by accepting the limitations of fair trade and moving on. Either way, we have a clear and achievable goal: to get everyone to green in everything.

Along those lines, time and again I've heard people ask me 'what happens when someone is green in everything?' Simply put: they become a member of the middle class. I know that 'middle class' is a loaded term, so let me explain how I'm using it. To be middle class is simply to be able to ask for what you want and need. To know how to take advantage of opportunities, to petition those in power and to compare your life to that of others. It's not about having a certain level of income, a certain type of job or a certain color of shirt collar. It's not about what you have but about demanding better for yourself because you know that it's worth it—and that it's possible.

WALMART. MY DREAM IS TO GET WALMART to join the Business Without Poverty program. I know what you're thinking. Walmart is traditionally painted (and perhaps not unfairly) as the archetypal evil corporation; one that is allergic to paying its workers a fair wage. I don't think this is too controversial a point to make: witness all of the evidence showing that Walmart workers are underpaid (both relative to other employers, and in absolute terms). Walmart Founder Sam Walton is on record stating that the company's success is built on a low-wage, low-benefit model. Given this, there is a lot of popular pressure for Walmart to increase worker wages.

And that seems like a good thing, on the face of it. But consider, for a moment, whether that knee-jerk reaction stems from the fact that you're living in the old paradigm—the one where poverty equals a lack of money and nothing else. If our lobbying efforts succeed and Walmart raises wages, will we go home, satisfied we've won the battle? Aren't we past the point where we believe that, if we just throw money at poverty, it will go away? Do we really believe that, if Walmart gave everyone a pay increase, all its workers would be green in everything? I know for a fact that they wouldn't because we see it all the time: people who are green in income but have a surprising number of reds and yellows in other indicators.

That's because income is the easy part. What I mean by this is that there are some relatively simple means of increasing a family's income, such as working more, having all family members over 18 generating income, getting a better education or more training, moving to a place with more (and more diverse) employment opportunities or opening a business. I'm not claiming that these are always easy to do, but there is a general understanding of the steps someone can take to increase their income, and these are things that can be learned. Instead, income is simply the counterintuitive tip of a very large iceberg that is often made up of booze, violence and a lack of stability, respect and family budget, among other things.

So maybe, just maybe, we condemn Walmart for its wage policy because we can't see that income isn't the real problem—or the only problem. Even if we solved the wage problem, if workers don't have a family budget, how can they be certain they're using their resources wisely? Or what if the problem is that workers don't have access to a car, so too much of that wage is spent on traveling to and from work, via public transportation that is infrequent and relatively more expensive? What if a domestic violence problem means the family member earning the wage isn't the one making decisions about how to allocate it? Would a higher wage address any of these underlying problems? Probably not.

That being the case—maybe, just maybe, Walmart doesn't know how many of its employees depend on welfare to get by. And what if Walmart could help all of its workers get to green in each indicator without raising wages one cent? I'm not suggesting for a moment that you stop condemning Walmart for its wage policy, or that it doesn't need to pay its workers more, because it does—but I am encouraging you to take a broader view. Living wages are important, but poverty is more than a lack of money. And whatever the case, a Walmart that knows the multidimensional needs of its workers (and increases worker productivity by addressing those needs) will always be better than a Walmart that doesn't.

I acknowledge that I've just raised a lot of challenging questions and concepts, and I'm certainly not claiming to have all the answers at this point. All I'm saying is that these are the kinds of conversations we can start to have once we have granular, multidimensional poverty maps for each family; once we can see how different deprivations interact and influence each other (or don't); once we can aggregate up to community level and start asking questions such as: 'Why do so many workers in this government agency not have a national ID card?' So much of our current economic thinking and practice is based on assumptions that were never correct in the first place. In so many ways, we need to start again at the beginning.

For that reason, I'm grateful that we started working at an organizational level to apply the Poverty Stoplight with concentrated groups of people, starting with *Fundación Paraguaya* itself. Doing so allowed us to ask questions about how deprivation plays out in people's lives in a way we simply couldn't have by applying it to a 10 percent random sample of clients scattered across the country. It allowed us to take a collective view of individual problems and identify the broader trends.

Most of all, it helped us see the role of the private sector in poverty elimination. Yes, the Poverty Stoplight is about giving poverty back to individuals—but it seemed to depend on having a skilled and motivated organization facilitating the process and doing the influencing. In the past, we'd encouraged government to take on that role—but it proved too inflexible. We'd encouraged development NGOs and civil society organizations to take on that role—but they were unable to make their single-issue solutions work in this new landscape of multidimensional poverty. But the private sector? It was agile, well-resourced and incentivized to promote employee well-being as a driver of productivity. A world of possibility seemed to be opening up—which surprised me, considering how deeply conservative Paraguayan businesses can be.

But I'm not just talking about big businesses here. In August of 2018, Luis Fernando knocked on the door of my office with some surprising news: "I forgot to tell you: since March, my team and I have been working on increasing the scope of the Business Without Poverty program. We've been using the Poverty Stoplight with our Village Bank microfinance clients, as you know—but we wondered what would happen if we included our individual loan clients as well? Many of them have employees of their own—with our support, they could become 'micro-businesses without poverty'. Just imagine an individual loan client, a seamstress maybe, who we support to do the Poverty Stoplight on herself and her two sewing assistants? What do you think?"

Cautious to the last, Luis Fernando had started with a small pilot: each Loan Officer would mentor 20 microentrepreneurs to help their own staff get to green. He wanted to reach 1,440 families in the first year: 924 clients surveying themselves, 85 of whom would in turn survey and support some 516 of their employees. The goal was to help 530 of those families get to green—either in income or in everything.

Given that it's usually me pitching audacious ideas to Luis Fernando, the role reversal here struck me as particularly poignant—and, of course, I was enthusiastic and support-ive. After all, if we wanted to harness the power of private business to eliminate poverty, we had to find a way to mean-ingfully include small and micro enterprises, which account for the majority of Paraguayan businesses.

All of this was exciting, but what if expanding outreach to small and large companies wasn't the best strategy? What if we actually didn't need anyone else? What if we didn't need governments, NGOs or private businesses to facilitate the poverty-elimination process? What if we put the Poverty Stoplight directly into the hands of families and cut out the middlemen entirely?

It was a question we'd get to answer sooner than we thought.

CHAPTER 14
POVERTY-FREE VILLAGES

IN 2016, EIGHT YEARS SINCE Luis Fernando challenged me to articulate what I meant by the word 'poverty', we paused to take stock of how far we'd come as a Foundation. In that time, we'd developed and applied the Poverty Stoplight to individual clients, to women in our microfinance groups, to Foundation staff and to the staff of other companies.

Each one of these experiences had taught us valuable lessons about how to define and facilitate social change—and all of them shared one critical defect: the families we were supporting weren't continually connected to each other in any sort of horizontal network. As a result, they weren't able to team up with each other to overcome their deprivations when we weren't around.

In short, our ability to create social sources of motivation and ability (to borrow Joseph Grenny's terms) was limited once our Stoplight participants returned home to their families after work or their monthly credit-group meetings. This was especially true for people in the Business Without Poverty programs, in which company mentors never came into contact with the family (unlike the mentors who visited microfinance clients in their homes, where they often met the clients' relations).

In the case of needs that arise at the family level (such as creating a family budget), the coaching and problem-solving that occur between the mentor and the head of the household can effectively impart the ideas, tools and motivation needed to tackle any issue. But let's face it: keeping a family budget isn't fun; it's tedious and time-consuming, and the payoffs are long term rather than short term (and, given the choice, we like our payoffs to be short term). So why bother at all?

This is where social sources of motivation come in handy. If everyone who lives on your street is keeping a family budget; if every time you visit a neighbor you see their family budget hanging from the wall; if, when you walk into the local shop, you have a conversation with the shopkeeper about how you're putting the money you would have spent on cake into a special fund for a new sewing machine—you change the conversation. You change the norms. If everyone is doing it, you'll do it too. Keeping a family budget becomes normal. Accepted. Encouraged. The example that your peers set has a profound influence on your individual choices, and will help us to demand better of ourselves. That's social motivation.

Likewise, social ability is important. Getting a whole community of people working together on a problem is a powerful thing. The Poverty Stoplight gives families something which I liken to a magnifying glass. It helps a family to articulate their needs for goods and services and then demand better from, for example, the government. When it comes to lobbying those external service providers to up their game, strength in numbers counts for a lot. Now imagine what would happen if we gave an entire community that magnifying glass. Think of the trapped energy we could unleash. It's the difference between one person in a community petitioning municipal officials to fix a potholed road and one hundred people making the same petition together.

ACKNOWLEDGING THIS, WE DEFINED our next bold challenge as a Foundation: to bring one entire community out of poverty within five years. What's more, we were going to try to do it without a project budget (apart from staff time), and to shape our activities entirely around community demand rather than our own priorities (in line with our methodology).

For the Foundation, it represented a thrilling opportunity to push the boundaries of knowledge and practice in poverty elimination—although I'm certain that most people thought we were crazy. After all, how can a community possibly know what's best for it? If they knew, surely they wouldn't be poor in the first place, right? Isn't it the job of the government to take care of them, anyway? And how can we eliminate poverty with zero budget—isn't ending poverty expensive? Isn't that why we have charity rock concerts to raise millions of dollars, as well as vociferous public debate about the high salaries of jet-setting development consultants and countless calls to prove, and improve, aid effectiveness and impact (read: value for money—lots of money)? And ending poverty is difficult and takes a long time, right? After all, the Millennium Development Goals (MDGs) had a timeline, and we definitely didn't hit our targets in time—which is why we needed to repackage them as the Sustainable Development Goals (SDGs). So trying to eliminate poverty in a community in five years is wishful thinking, pure and simple.

Perhaps those are all valid criticisms if your point of reference is the conventional development paradigm. But since we'd started using the Poverty Stoplight, the types of conversations we are able to have about poverty have changed fundamentally. We suspected, and hoped to discover, that there were synergies to be found when an entire community went through the same process at once.

One of these might be that we'd be able to replace poverty traps with poverty trampolines. When I say 'poverty traps', I am talking about the perverse incentives poor families face that make staying in poverty the most rational choice, given all their options. We wanted to know whether we could replace these with a set of new incentives telling poor families that eliminating their deprivations was, in fact, the most attractive option. And, let me tell you, we'd seen plenty of poverty traps in action over the years.

Take, for instance, a microfinance client in the town of Coronel Oviedo who, after taking the visual survey, prioritized getting from red to green in 'Modern Bathroom'. She took out a home-improvement loan and replaced her pit latrine with a beautiful new bathroom—but she built it ten feet away from her actual house, situated in a neighboring garden belonging to a relative. Why so far away? Because her welfare payments from the government would stop if they knew she had enough money to do home improvements. It's a laughable scenario, but this woman was acting in a perfectly rational manner, given the circumstances—given her environment.

Conversely, by including every member of a community on a shared quest to overcome poverty – a journey in which having problems was nothing to be ashamed of, solving problems was something to celebrate and supporting each other to solve problems was normal – we hoped to create a shared spirit of optimism and a culture of achievement. We'd seen this time and again in our agricultural high schools, where our students achieved more than they ever thought possible—because the environment was designed to support and promote that achievement. *Change the environment, change the outcomes.*

Second, by taking the Poverty Stoplight door to door to every home in one community, we were hoping to unleash trapped resources that families could share with other families. We had always known that different families are rarely all poor in the same ways or to the same extent—and that all of them are non-poor in ways that are just as various. But now, thanks to technology, we'd be able to create 'heat maps' for every indicator. In other words, by superimposing our survey data onto a satellite map of the neighborhood and slicing that data by indicator, we would be able to pinpoint, down to the house number, any individual greens swimming in a sea of reds. If a family needed to improve their nutrition, we could point them to the nearest family that was beating the odds on the issue. Similarly, we as a Foundation would be able to ask ourselves really detailed and practical questions about aggregate outcome differentials – such as: 'Why are families in the north end of this community poorer in garbage than at the south end?' – and start a conversation with the community on what the best solution might be.

Most importantly, we were hoping to put the 'community' back into 'community development'. Just like a family can own its own poverty, a community can as well—and, when they don't, 'community development' projects will always fail. The fact of the matter is that governments deliver top-down, one-size-fits-all community development projects because they don't have any other choice. They don't have the data they need to do anything else. The farthest the government can 'see' into a community is through the lens of an extractive survey: the government defines its own indicators, collects its own data and aggregates that data into percentages. Nowhere is there room for the perspective of individual families, and so government departments allocate budgets based on gross generalizations: 35 percent of kids aren't in school; 45 percent of villagers don't have water. But if you ask: '*Which* kids aren't in school?' or '*Which* families don't have water?' the government doesn't know—its accountability stops at building a school, building a well.

And even when the government takes the time to engage in community consultation, the process is usually consensus-driven, meaning any recommendations that emerge from the process will be of *general agreed benefit* to the entire community: a new bus stop, a new stop sign at an intersection, a new road to market. While these things are, of course, valuable, the community group doesn't have granular information about the needs that exist *within* individual families, and families aren't always self-aware or confident enough to articulate those needs.

As a result, the government might, for example, in response to community feedback, build a new health post—without any understanding of which families have what health needs and why. And if the post is built but no one uses it, the assumption is that people are too stupid or too lazy to take charge of their health—even if the real reasons are that they are afraid to visit the doctor, or unaware of their health needs, or unable to get to the clinic without support. This isn't a hypothetical example that I've invented out of thin air; Paraguay is littered with community development projects that didn't work out as planned.

Information is power. So, for the Foundation, the question became: what would happen if we gave a community the power it needed to eliminate its own poverty? We were about to find out.

We'd taken steps in this direction before, with the Curuguaty Plan in 2012, and were determined to learn from that experience. Curuguaty was a government-led project with social workers from different agencies and ministries deployed throughout the local community. In hindsight, we recognized two key shortcomings with this approach: First, communities equate government projects with hand-outs (free goods and services). Second, the change in government meant there was no follow-up. This time, we wanted to do 'community development with teeth': real accountability for results (not just activities and outputs) in the short and medium term, and a poverty-elimination initiative that paid for itself (similar to our microfinance and agricultural education programs) so we wouldn't need a project budget.

As for where we'd work, the choice of community was easy. The Cerrito community contained over 1,000 households, and the Foundation had been a familiar (and respected) presence there since we took over the agricultural school in 2003. Moreover, the community itself contained interesting economic and ethnic diversity: families from three different groups of the same *Qom* indigenous tribe and families living at all levels of income poverty, many in extreme poverty. For the purposes of testing the Poverty Stoplight at the community level, we had our work cut out for us.

BUILDING THE RIGHT TEAM would be essential, and was our first step to getting this initiative underway. We approached two people with the courage and vision we needed: Fernando Pfannl and Celsa Acosta. Fernando had previously served as Senator, National Planning Minister and our country's Ambassador to the US during the Obama administration. Celsa's vocation lay in education (she first joined our team as Administrator of the Cerrito Agricultural High School, so she had a deep familiarity with the community), but she had also headed the national government's anti-poverty agency. Both had solid social justice credentials—and, more importantly, both were willing to embrace our non-traditional approach and construct a 'bottom-up', family-led community poverty-eradication initiative. We also recruited and trained five social workers, who would each handle a portfolio of about 200 families, as our mentors. They were hired from outside the community—it felt vital that they be seen as objective and impartial so that families could confidently discuss their challenges with them. To this team, we added two Foundation staff members—two women, from indigenous communities, to act as 'cultural translators' and help us raise awareness and set expectations with *Qom* leaders and families.

Next, we had to find the families. At first, we were dismayed to learn that the local municipality didn't actually have up-to-date land maps of the area. In classic 'silver lining' style, however, we were able to create custom-made digital maps using (of all things) drones. In Paraguay, drones are in frequent use for agricultural and forestry purposes, and we were able to identify an inexpensive consultant to map the town in a single day. We used our new maps to record the position of not only each household but also each local public facility (such as health posts, schools and roads), community group, facility (churches, football pitches and parks), NGO and business. This allowed us to understand what groups and existing resources we could work with as part of the initiative.

Having mapped where everyone was, it was time to go talk to them. We wanted to meet with each individual family in the community to talk about the potential benefits of the initiative. Throughout this process, our constant refrain would be that we weren't in the business of giving charity. We weren't doing state welfare. Nor was this project going to be led by traditional community leaders—we'd be working directly with families.

That being said, we contacted each traditional community leader first to get their blessing. Cerrito was a complex political microcosm, and conducting the initial approach correctly would be important. Here's why: Cerrito can be divided into two distinct communities—indigenous and non-indigenous (or Paraguayans, as the indigenous people call us). Within the non-indigenous community, there are 24 different community leaders, typically approved by the city government and associated with particular neighborhoods, churches and sports clubs. What's more, within the indigenous part of the village, there are four different chiefs from three indigenous *Qom* communities. Although each of them belongs to the same ethnic group or tribe, the indigenous communities are divided into different settlements because they come from different areas of the country. If this initiative was going to work, everyone needed to be on board.

In the end, we were pleasantly surprised that three out of four *Qom* chiefs gave us their blessing to approach the families unaccompanied—even when they had their doubts about the initiative. Perhaps that remark deserves a bit of explanation: when I say we were pleasantly surprised, it's because indigenous tribes are (with just cause, given our national history) cautious and suspicious when it comes to outside interference. What's more, given that our intention was to work directly with families, there was every possibility that the chiefs might have viewed our work as a threat to their position as formal intermediaries between their people and the outside world (not just government, but society as a whole).

I suspect (but cannot prove) that getting the chiefs on board had something to do with the fact that the Foundation had, over the years, built up reputation capital and goodwill within the community. Or maybe we were allowed a high level of autonomy within the community because we reassured the chiefs about the initiative's own autonomy. Money plays a big role in this. Part of our insistence on running this initiative with a budget of zero was for pragmatic reasons: we wanted to get started, rather than to be held captive by unpredictable donor grant-making decision cycles. Also, since we weren't building anything or providing new services, we didn't have any real costs—other than staff time, which we felt was ours alone to shoulder. More importantly, however, outside money always comes with an outside agenda. Whether the money is from the government, a donor or a private foundation, there are always conditions attached—implicit and explicit. If the Cerrito project was truly to be a community-led initiative, we didn't want any external forces shaping what we were trying to do and why.

In addition to the tribal chiefs, we sat down with the leaders of different churches, neighborhood committees, military detachments and schools. In total, this community engagement and awareness-raising process lasted approximately three months.

As we laid the groundwork for the Cerrito initiative, we had high hopes that we'd see valuable results. To help us put those results into some sort of meaningful context, we did something we'd never done before: we created a control (comparison) group. We selected a nearby community, with similar economic opportunities and characteristics, called *Tierra Prometida* (Promised Land). With the families in this community, we used a different style of survey (no pictures, no colors, no results dashboard for the family to keep and no mentoring). Here's why: we wanted to gather the same quantity and type of information, but we wanted to do so without the process triggering any sort of awareness raising or action planning on the part of the family. (That might sound harsh—and maybe it is. One of the things that makes me uneasy about social impact assessments is when they rely on the use of a control group of people – who are poor enough to qualify for support, but who you refused to help – so that you can measure what would have happened to the people you are helping, had you chosen not to help them at all.)

The baseline survey of the Cerrito community was carried out over the course of two weekends. We approached 1,069 families; of these, 891 agreed to be surveyed. Of the remaining 178 families, 90 families were not at home that weekend, 27 said they didn't want to participate, 24 said they didn't have time and 3 said they didn't have approval from

their village leader. A further 34 families chose not to participate without signaling why.

When we compiled the results, the scale of the challenge
snapped into clear focus. In my country, 24 percent of the
overall population lives in income poverty (36 percent in rural
areas). For the members of the Cerrito community, that figure jumps to 53 percent. And, while 5 percent of Paraguayans
overall (and 9 percent of the rural population) live in extreme
poverty, in Cerrito that figure is 37 percent.

For the indigenous *Qom* families in Cerrito (who make up
61 percent of the community), the picture is even bleaker:
65 percent live in poverty and 48 percent live in extreme
poverty. This last finding, in particular, paid grim tribute
to the 'separate and (un)equal' system that is the reality in
Paraguay. In 1981, Congress passed Law 904 (the Statute of
Indigenous Communities), which was intended to protect
indigenous communities but which, in reality, created a
system of apartheid. Indigenous tribes have their own government agency, schools and health posts (which deliver a
very poor quality of service) and are typically not welcome to
access non-indigenous government services. Looking at non-
income indicators only reinforces the point: *Qom* families
were less likely to save, less likely to have decent garbage-
disposal facilities and good nutrition, less likely to take care
of their eyes and teeth and more likely to lack a bathroom.

The Cerrito survey results also confirmed what we were
seeing elsewhere: income wasn't the main problem. More
to the point, a lack of income wasn't driving deprivations
in other areas. So, while 53 percent of community members scored themselves as red in 'Income', that apparently
wasn't stopping them from having access to 'Potable Water'
or 'Vaccines' (each 3 percent red), 'Electricity' and good
'Personal Hygiene' (each 6 percent red), 'Sufficient Clothing'
and an 'Entrepreneurial Spirit' (16 percent red each).
What's more: 74 percent of families were green in 'Phone',

yet fewer than half of families scored themselves green in 'Access to Credit' (35 percent) and fewer than a quarter did so in 'Income' (24 percent). Overall, the only indicators that ranked worse than 'Income' in Cerrito (53 percent red) were 'Savings' (81 percent red), 'Budget' and 'Garbage Disposal' (65 percent red each).*

Now for the shocking news: after they'd completed their visual survey and taken stock of their strengths and weaknesses, families prioritized sorting out their savings situations and garbage disposal more often than they did increasing their family income. This is true in both relative and absolute terms: 417 families prioritized 'Savings', which works out as 74 percent of families that scored red or yellow in savings. Likewise, 198 out of the 499 families (or 40 percent) that were red or yellow in 'Garbage Disposal' made this a top priority, whereas only 30 percent of families that were red or yellow in 'Income' made increasing their income a priority (144 out of 474 families).

It's one thing for the Foundation to claim that income isn't the problem, but it's quite another to hear that message echoed by the families themselves. When we talked to villagers about this, we heard stories about having nowhere safe to keep any occasional cash they might get from selling handicrafts. Savings accounts were also a relatively novel concept for the community, which might explain why this indicator felt more compelling to community members. In terms of 'Garbage Disposal', we should consider that community members' strong emphasis on this indicator might have been related to ongoing public information campaigns about dengue-fever prevention (inasmuch as the rainwater that collects in discarded drinks bottles, tin cans, tires and other forms of rubbish around the house and property provide

---

*While we did 871 initial surveys, we only completed 626 follow-up surveys. Also, only 30 indicators were comparable between the two (the others were updated, making strict comparison impossible).

the perfect breeding ground for mosquitoes). By the same token, it's also a question of access to garbage-disposal services: a high proportion of the community was indigenous, and government garbage-disposal services (which had been privatized in Cerrito) didn't reach indigenous areas (because they couldn't pay for it).

With the surveys done, and the family plans in place, the mentoring phase was ready to begin. We worked at two levels: the group and the household. At both levels, we helped families to leverage existing resources (both inside the community and external resources) and to create new ones (new community resources, or working with external service providers to create new services).

In so many ways, the power to leverage existing but untapped community resources is the real beauty of having a detailed poverty map. Here's why: in theory, we know that – for any given indicator in any given community – there will be someone beating the odds. Conventional aggregated poverty data hints at this when it tells us, for instance, that 55 percent of a community has no access to health care. The obvious question to ask here is: what are the other 45 percent doing to access health care that most people in that community aren't? Sadly, conventional poverty data can't provide an answer; its insights are limited to overall percentages. On the other hand, the Poverty Stoplight can show us, down to the household level, who is beating the odds and in what. Because of this, our mentors have the data they need to connect leaders and laggards for each indicator. If a family scores red in a certain indicator and makes it a top priority on their Life Map, within moments their mentor can look up information on who they know within the community who might be green, and who can give them the guidance and encouragement they need to succeed.

So, for instance, two neighbors on the same street might have known each other for years, but have never discussed things like affordable bricks or school supplies before—but now our data allows us to spot that, if we pair up these families, they each have valuable insights and experiences to offer the other. One knows how to navigate the complex bureaucracy of the local water company to get connected to running water at home; the other knows how to monetize a knack for making willow baskets. One has a cousin who works at the building-supply store; the other has a nephew who knows how to de-louse poultry. All we need to do is connect people who have information with people who need information, and they do the rest.

Creating new community groups worked much in the same way: we were able to identify which *Qom* families derived a part of their income from handicrafts, for instance, and bring everyone together into one group to deliver business trainings, or help them apply for government cultural funding earmarked for indigenous groups. As part of our microfinance work, we were already well-versed in group formation and training; in Cerrito, we used the same skill set to create seven different indigenous artisan groups (of 25–40 members each).

We also offered Cerrito community members the opportunity to get involved in existing Foundation programs. A total of 45 women joined our microfinance program, 5 people signed up to our microfranchise program and we teamed up with the Paraguayan Microfinance Network to hold 2 entrepreneurship workshops for 190 people.

We also worked with the community to identify common needs that could be best met by government agencies, NGOs or businesses in the area. For instance, our mentors supported villagers to submit a written request to the Identification Department of the National Police to arrange a massive documentation exercise in the community. In one week alone, 180 people in Cerrito obtained their National Identity Card (required if you want to access government services, bank

203

loans and land titles) and 80 people, ranging from infants to septuagenarians, were issued a birth certificate.

In a similar way, we're supporting the local *Qom* community to engage with the National Indigenous Institute to access services and funding. For instance, as part of the mass documentation exercise, 612 people obtained their Indigenous Artisans Card (which opens up access to national expositions and markets). What's more, we're working along-side the *Qom* to secure Institute funding for a reforestation project that will both improve the local environment (by replanting and managing 200 hectares of unused land) and provide a sustainable stream of community income (from the sale of wood and forestry products). In these types of activi-ties, our mentors meet with community leaders to discuss the options, and the community leaders take the decision on how to proceed. Sometimes the community leaders will verbally dictate their petitions to the mentors, who type them up for approval.

In other cases, the villagers task us with negotiating with third-party organizations on their behalf, where we are better positioned to leverage our size and reputation as a Foundation. This is true for the example of savings. As mentioned earlier, through the Life Map exercise, 74 percent of families in Cerrito who scored red or yellow in 'Savings' identified this as a priority area. The problem was that there were simply no banks nearby. The community had articulated a problem, but our mentors were at a loss as to how to connect them to an existing solution. The nearest bank was 10 miles away; quite apart from clients' concerns over safely traveling that distance with large amounts of cash, once at the bank they are faced with lengthy and complicated paperwork just to open an account (in Spanish, which might be their second or third language), stringent requirements around proving the provenance of any monies deposited and a mandatory $500 minimum savings balance—all for a paltry interest rate of below 1 percent. Closer to home, Vision Bank offered a microsavings product with friendlier terms and conditions (no initial balance, no minimum savings requirements)—but the product was only offered to women (whereas in our traditionally *machista* culture, the men are typically in charge of family money matters).

So, we teamed up with Tigo (a local mobile-phone operator) and El Comercio (a local financial service provider) to design an entirely new solution. To our delight (considering how unusual our proposal was), both companies jumped at the chance to get involved. Here's how it works: families buy credit from the cell-phone network provider at one of any number of local kiosks, and then 'send' their credit via text message to the bank, which agreed to pay out 8 percent in interest if families leave their savings untouched for a minimum of six months. The minimum balance is only $1.50.

The initial concept seems promising, and we're very much following a 'learning by doing' approach to refine the model. Several important insights appeared early on. First, we needed to put more time than anticipated into training older people, who weren't familiar with using a smartphone and needed help from their children or grandchildren to use the smartphone app. This became a problem where grandparents had previously had bad experiences when their relatives got hold of their savings. Their reticence was understandable, and our hope was that the very nature of the Cerrito initiative would alleviate these concerns. More concretely, by getting every family in a community working toward the same clear goal at once (and seeing that success is within reach), we can eliminate the 'scarcity mindset' that might have led to young people filching money from unwitting relatives.

Villagers also invited the Planning Secretariat (the government body responsible for combating poverty) to introduce its savings groups methodology in Cerrito. Groups of 15 women receive five training sessions at the beginning of the program to learn how to manage the group and to assign leadership roles (president, secretary, treasurer, syndicate and others). Each woman is required to save at least $1.50 every week, an amount which is distributed equally into three accounts identified by a unique color: green for general savings that can be used however they want; yellow for 'social' savings to be used on health, education and the like; and red for emergency needs. No external bank is needed; the group is self-managing and self-operating, in charge of storing its own funds (in a triple-locked safe box) and keeping its own accounts (in a special booklet provided by the Secretariat).

To improve the security situation in and around Cerrito, a group of neighbors organized a Neighborhood Watch Commission. At their request, we connected them with the National Police and the Protek Foundation (an organization that promotes better citizen security) to undergo group training workshops. Afterward, community members developed their own initiatives, such as making their own 'Neighborhood Watch' signs and posting them in visible places to alert potential thieves to the efforts of the group. They also established a WhatsApp messaging group to notify each other when they spot suspicious persons about or to ask for help in the face of developing threats. They added the local office of the National Police to the WhatsApp group so it could to respond quickly to the needs of the community.

AS I WRITE, WE ARE ONE YEAR into the Cerrito initiative, and the jury is still out on whether we'll achieve our audacious goal of bringing an entire community out of poverty within five years. I can, however, share some interesting things we've witnessed so far.

First and foremost, we celebrate the individual accomplishments of community members such as Blanca. For her, getting to green in 'Income' was the main priority; her husband lost his job when he lost his sight, so Blanca set up her own ice-cream sales microfranchise (through a Foundation program) and now runs promotions on Facebook. Her next challenge is to improve her bathroom situation, which, despite being a modern facility, is located some distance from her house. Not only that, but she's joined a women's committee and helps to motivate other women in the community to get to green. Then there's Esteban, an indigenous neighborhood leader and single father, who is not only using his Poverty Stoplight and Life Map to work on his own challenges but also mentoring young addicts in the community and actively participating in the neighborhood commission.

There are countless stories such as these —of people not only unleashing their energy and creativity to solve the problems they identify but also reaching out into the community to support others to do the same thing. If we subscribed to popular mythology about the general apathy and ineptitude of the poor, we'd be at a loss to explain any of this. However, for us, stories such as those of Blanca and Esteban simply confirm that, with the right information and tools, poor individuals can and will demand more of themselves—and help their neighbors do the same.

So, too, do we hear stories of people who, once they start turning their reds and yellows into greens, are motivated to keep going. It's not unusual to talk to people who describe the benefit of getting to green in a certain indicator in terms of the realization that there are other related areas they could improve. Successfully solving one problem, it seems, gives us the confidence boost we need to solve another, and another, and so on.

What's more, if you talked to the Cerrito team they would tell you that, while they have been busy doing continuous mentoring and organizing group activities, at least 80 percent of the improvements have occurred without any input from them at all. The Cerrito they walk through today is much different from the Cerrito of a year ago – more activated, more optimistic – and, while our mentors definitely feel part of that change, they won't take the credit for it.

It's not just anecdotes such as these that give me cause for hope. Thanks to the second visual survey (carried out nine months after the first), we now have real data on what's going on in Cerrito—about how the landscape of poverty is changing, and what challenges still remain.

Over the course of 9 months, members of the Cerrito community successfully eliminated 1,066 reds and gained 631 greens and 435 yellows. Between them, 189 families added up to 8 greens each, and 76 families added up to 21 greens each. The biggest overall drop was in reds (6 percent), two-thirds of which became green. In total, 346 families improved to green or yellow in 'Comfortable Home'; 340 families made similar progress in 'Vaccines', 314 families in 'Child Labor', 293 in 'Income' and 281 in 'Sexual Health'. Indigenous families improved at a far more rapid rate than non-indigenous families (on which more later).

Certainly, no discussion about what's been happening in Cerrito would be complete without talking about what we've observed in *Tierra Prometida*. On average, the families in our comparison group were more or less the same by the second survey, averaging 17 greens in 2017 and 15 in 2018. While 'Income' greens increased from 40 to 47 percent, 'Access to Credit' greens tailed off a little (from 35 to 34 percent) and 'Savings' greens dropped from 10 to 3 percent.

Back in Cerrito, the second visual survey also revealed some surprising reversals of fortune compared to the first. First off, the number of 'Accessible Roads' greens dropped by 85, and most of these (81) became red. We suspect that doing the second survey 9 months later, rather than 12, meant this result was driven by seasonal changes rather than actual changes in infrastructure. If that proves to be the case, it's a good lesson for us in terms of how context drives people's perception of their own poverty—and how deprivations can be more, or less, visible given the circumstances.

Two other reversals deserve mention here. First, 'Access to Health Post' greens in Cerrito dropped by 202, yellows increased by 173 and reds increased by 29. Second, among the 190 non-indigenous Cerrito families, 'Domestic Violence' greens slipped from 184 to 181. What was happening here? Did the local health station suddenly get further away or curtail its open hours? Did three non-indigenous husbands start abusing their wives? In terms of health, it's worth noting that, between the two surveys, our research team tweaked the indicator to encompass not just proximity to the health post but also the quality of services available there. Given that the clinic is underfunded and poorly equipped, the second result is likely a better reflection of what's actually happening on the ground. In terms of domestic violence, it's worth asking whether the violence itself increased or families' awareness of it, such that things that didn't seem like a problem before suddenly were. If that is the case, we should welcome this increased awareness (inasmuch as it's the first step toward addressing a problem), rather than lament the trend emerging in the data.

PERHAPS MORE INTERESTING THAN our activities or interim survey results, however, are the lessons that we, as a development organization, are learning from this experience—insights about poverty, and about applying the Poverty Stoplight, that haven't emerged in other places where we are using the methodology with clients or companies.

The first surprise is about relationships. We were surprised to find that the relationship between our mentors and the families in the Cerrito community is much more fluid and informal than in other contexts. This is because the mentors spend the majority of their working week in and around Cerrito. Thus, while the methodology calls for a monthly visit with each family, the reality is that the contact with families is much more frequent and *ad hoc*. For instance, a villager might spot the mentor calling in on their neighbor, or walking down the road, and take advantage of the situation to ask for advice or give them an update on a situation. Our mentors also report that they are routinely invited to attend community and family celebrations—so much so that they are starting to feel a welcomed part of the village; embedded support rather than external advisors.

We're also finding that we devote a lot of time and care to fostering quality relationships between the community and third-party organizations, such as local government, local companies, NGOs and civic groups. We do this first and foremost in an educational capacity: making villagers aware of existing support and resources that they can draw on when they need to. We also facilitate direct contact, by inviting other organizations to relevant meetings and events and using the power of our convening role to help the community build stronger networks, which it can draw on for support in the future. This not only helps villagers to find the confidence to engage with outside organizations but also makes those organizations more aware of the needs and interests of the community.

The second surprise is about solutions. In the bank of solutions we had been compiling over the course of years, we found a critical lack of solutions that were appropriate at the group level. This gap is understandable, since before we arrived in Cerrito we were working with families one at a time. There's a word we use, borrowed from the *Guaraní* language, to describe these group activities: *mingas*. This term connotes doing things together as a community, such as agreeing to all get together on a Tuesday to re-seed the grass on the local soccer field.

On the one hand, it's fantastic that we get to add lots of new types of solutions to our catalog. On the other hand, it begs the question: are we spending too much time on group activities rather than individual accompaniment? I'm not sure there's an answer to that question. Certainly, Joseph Grenny would remind us that we should be activating all sources of influence (at the social, individual and structural levels) at once. But at the end of the day, the methodology stipulates that we take a demand-driven approach. We can bring options to the table in terms of how to tackle any given challenge, but the final decision rests with the community, and it's our job to follow their lead. Given this, I'm tempted to say that if the community was agreeing on group-based activities in light of all the options, then it was probably the correct approach.

The third surprise is around priorities. I've already painted a picture of the challenges facing Cerrito, in terms of the deprivations and isolation felt by the community, and how these are more keenly felt by the indigenous sections of the community. How that reality would shape our priorities, the priorities of the villagers and the priorities of local government came as something of a shock, however.

In terms of our own outlook, I'm not sure we could have anticipated how our mentors would react to differing levels of need within a concentrated community. Our initial survey revealed the stark truth about the 'separate but (un)equal' system that has locked our indigenous tribes out of society and out of opportunity. In the first survey, Cerrito's indigenous families had over twice as many reds, on average, as non-indigenous families (9 versus 4, respectively). In terms of yellows, indigenous families averaged 6, while non-indigenous averaged 4. Greens? 15 versus 22. Sixty percent of indigenous families were red in 'Income', whereas only 33 percent of non-indigenous families were red in 'Income'.

As the months unfolded, however, our mentors noticed they were spending a lot more time with indigenous families.

Why was this happening? There was nothing in the methodology stipulating that every family was to receive the same amount of contact time with the mentors—and, as already mentioned, that contact was happening in a much more fluid, ongoing and informal way than we had ever experienced before. So what was driving this difference? Was it that mentors were deliberately focusing their efforts on the areas of greatest perceived need? Was it an unconscious choice? Was the indigenous community simply more demanding of our mentors' time and attention? We cannot say for certain.

What we do know, however, is that the second survey revealed that the indigenous community is making significant strides—and the non-indigenous community appears to be going backward. Average reds fell by three per indigenous household, whereas average reds rose by one in non-indigenous households. Indigenous greens rose by three per household, whereas non-indigenous greens fell by three. Without further research, and without taking into account mitigating factors (heavy flooding, an outbreak of dengue and a slight change to the health-post indicator, among others), we can't draw any firm conclusions on why these results occurred. But it's a good reminder to our team to be mindful of how we allocate our time and attention within the entire community in a way that balances everyone's needs and priorities.

Here's another point about priorities: sometimes the community's priorities change. As I mentioned, our mentoring methodology is centered around their priorities, not ours. We can advise; we can influence; but it's not our job to decide. So, when the community initially decided that garbage removal was a key priority, we jumped into action by discussing potential solutions. The key barrier was that the government privatized garbage collection, and residents are required to pay $4 per month for weekly service. Some people (especially in the indigenous community) simply didn't see the importance of garbage collection, preferring to burn their garbage (plastics and all) in the garden every day. Other villagers, who wanted this service but couldn't afford it, spoke of their frustration in seeing the garbage truck pass them by every week on its way to collect someone else's waste.

We were hopeful that, with the right information and motivation, we could move the needle on garbage habits in the village. We were especially hopeful that villagers would take advantage of their increased incomes to get to green in garbage. Only they didn't. Yes – incomes went up – but for some reason we don't fully understand, that didn't translate into the community making good on its stated intention. For some reason, they lost interest. And, while we might not have wanted to do so, we took our foot off the pedal on this issue. We'll come back to it when the time is right, but in the interim we've been using our time wisely, exploring the possibility of negotiating different service levels with the local municipality (for instance, fortnightly collections of only non-organic waste for $1 per month).

Our time in Cerrito has also helped us take a different view of the government's priorities, as seen through the lens of government anti-poverty programs. Housing is a perfect case in point here. Near the Cerrito community, the government is building new social-housing units for poor families. On the face of things, public housing seems like a really great solution to help low-income families who can't afford to build or buy their own. Each government housing unit cost $13,000 to build. Sounds pretty good, right? Maybe, maybe not—because here's another example of how using the Poverty Stoplight changes the kinds of conversations we can have about poverty.

Let's start with the basics: the Poverty Stoplight has seven different indicators related to housing. These include having a safe roof, windows and doors; separate bedrooms for adults and children; elevated stove and ventilated kitchen; a modern bathroom; refrigerator and other appliances; furniture and household utensils; and electricity. Half of all the families we initially surveyed in Cerrito had three or fewer housing deprivations, and only one-third of families had more than five. The average number of housing deprivations was 3.4. After the visual survey, 262 families named various types of housing improvements as top priorities on their Life Maps. On average, families needed $2,000 to resolve their housing issues—in other words, $2,000 to be non-poor in housing.

The numbers speak for themselves. Had the government approached these 262 families with an offer of social housing, the cost to the government would have been $3.4 million, instead of the $524,000 that was actually needed to get everyone's housing indicators to green. In other words, for a fraction of the cost, the government could shift its focus from building new housing stock to making existing housing stock fit for purpose—fixing what's broken, rather than starting over from scratch. Beyond just the cost savings involved, it would mean people could stay in their own homes and communities rather than being relocated. Surely a better policy, therefore, would be to invest in improved housing within communities?

Of course, without the comprehensive family-level data on individual housing deprivations needed to make that happen, it would be a laughable suggestion. (By way of a sidebar, the National Housing Agency recently approached us about replicating the Cerrito 'Village Without Poverty' initiative with the 900 members of the government housing project of Barrio San Francisco—a powerful reminder that solving just one piece of the multidimensional poverty puzzle, housing, isn't sufficient.)

I'll leave you with a final thought here. Our Cerrito experience, while still unfolding, has demonstrated that raising awareness about poverty doesn't occur at the same rate as raising awareness about poverty traps. I have yet to meet a poor person who doesn't understand their own poverty. Everyone knows where their shoes pinch when they walk in them every day. What's harder to visualize is how a different pair of shoes, or maybe a different way of walking, might make the journey more comfortable. Within a very short time, we have witnessed incredible progress within the indigenous community—between the first and second survey, they halved (or more than halved) the number of reds in terms of 'Income', 'Credit', 'Clean Environment', 'Personal Hygiene', 'Sexual Health', 'Secure Home', 'Comfortable Home', 'Adequate Clothing', 'Electricity', 'Entrepreneurial Spirit' and 'Access to Transport'. In the 'Conscious of Our Own Needs' indicator, the number of reds fell from 142 to 34.

Despite this, our mentors are keenly aware of entrenched poverty traps within the indigenous community that the members of that community cannot yet see for themselves. For instance, Fernando reports that each month there are two days on which the mentors cannot hold any meetings with indigenous families—because they're not at home. Like clockwork, the heads of household have gone off to Villa Hayes (a town situated 10 miles away) to collect their monthly government welfare check.

Is this a profitable use of their time? Not even close. Between the cost of getting there by bus ($2–3), the cost of food for the trip (another $2–3) and the opportunity cost of not working for a couple of days every month ($15 per day, assuming they're earning minimum wage) while they're walking to the bus, waiting for the bus, traveling to town, going to the welfare office and standing in the line at a bank to cash the check, they've potentially thrown away between $21 and $36—all so they can collect a $40 welfare check. Literally and figuratively, it just doesn't add up. Yet as Paulo Freire and Ken Wilber would remind us: We cannot force them to see what we see. We cannot simply plug our knowledge into their heads. All we can do is help them to climb the ladder of their own consciousness.

All in all, it's a journey that is ongoing. This is true not only for the community, as it learns the ways in which it can flex its muscle to overcome its deprivations, but also for us as a Foundation, as we learn about the Poverty Stoplight by implementing the Poverty Stoplight. We are hopeful that we are on the right path—and interested to see how the lessons and insights emerging from our experience help other development organizations to climb their own ladder toward more effective poverty-eradication initiatives.

REFLECTIONS

MARCH 27, 2018. MY HEART was once more in my throat as I ascended the steps of the National Development Bank in downtown Asunción. I paused in front of the oversized brass doors, reflecting on how much had changed since I last passed through them. The building was no longer tattooed with the name of our erstwhile dictator in neon lights, but the sight and sounds of the street vendors in the square below were much the same. It was 36 years since I had been fired from my job at the Ministry of Industry and Commerce for refusing to affiliate myself with the Colorado Party, and 33 years since I had been laughed out of the office of the Manager of the National Development Bank, clutching my business plan and more hope than certainty that the Foundation would ever find the money needed to get off the ground.

In the intervening decades, my team and I had presided over a quiet but essential revolution—and not a political one, the fear of which meant that Stroessner and his secret police were a constant (if not obvious) presence in our client meetings until he was finally deposed in 1989. Instead, the Foundation presided over a social revolution—one in which we found a way to give poverty back to poor people.

In many ways, my meeting with the National Development Bank Manager was an important catalyst for this whole story—inasmuch as it forced us to embrace, from the outset, the hard truth that the Foundation's work would fly in the face of development orthodoxy. That conversation, my confusion at his inability to see the merits of a bottom-up approach to tackling poverty, my revulsion at hearing poor people described as 'the plague'—all this affirmed my belief in pursuing the course of action I felt was right, rather than what was popular.

Yet the National Development Bank had also, in my mind, come to symbolize something more: a deep faith that change is possible. The fact that I was standing on the steps gazing up at those doors was the proof. I was there at the invitation of the National Development Bank, which was interested in joining the Foundation's Business Without Poverty initiative to eliminate poverty among its own staff.

I am not ashamed to admit that I cherish moments such as these—moments where we can visibly see that the work of the Foundation is gaining traction in arenas where, in the past, it drew criticism. And honestly, if we don't take the time to cherish these things, then it's far too easy to look out at the world and succumb to a deep sense of pessimism about whether or not we will ever win the fight against global poverty.

There are countless organizations working hard, working every day, to create social and economic justice in the world. You may work for one of them. You may support one of them through donations of your time or money.

The ecosystem created by these organizations is vast and complex. They include impact investors, national development banks, bilateral and multilateral donor organizations, government ministries, philanthropic foundations, registered charities, voluntary associations, civil society organizations, citizens advice services, private consulting firms, research bodies, social rating agencies, academic institutions, networks, NGOs, social enterprises, lobbying firms, political action committees, boycott organizers, student protest groups, advocacy organizations and social movements.

No such list can ever be complete. Nor does it need to be to make the point that, for all the hours and dollars being thrown at the problem of global poverty, it's hard to avoid the sneaking suspicion that we should have worked ourselves out of a job by now; that there's something standing in between us and total poverty elimination—and that part of the problem might be us.

The solution I offer to this challenge exists within a moment of profound social, political, economic and technological change. Old paradigms are falling by the wayside and new ones are emerging, powered by technology, as well as a more diverse set of voices in the spaces where debates are held and decisions are made. These new ways of doing things affect every aspect of our lives: the ways in which we live, eat, work and play; the ways in which we collaborate; the ways in which we hold our leaders accountable; the ways in which we envision the world that we want to leave to our children.

So, too, does the Poverty Stoplight exist in a moment when radical thinkers and writers are challenging us to re-think the shape of economic theory and development practice. We are called to re-orient our economies toward the sweet spot that lies between the double cliff edges of environmental degradation and human deprivation. So, too, are we called to design poverty-elimination programs that are powered by the insights of the real experts on poverty: not the people sitting in the boardroom but the people living in the slums. We are called upon to envision programs that facilitate poverty elimination by the people and for the people. Whereas these thinkers trace the topography of this new landscape of possibility, the Poverty Stoplight offers a potentially useful means of navigating through that landscape.

WE ONLY NEED TWO THINGS to achieve a radical vision for total and lasting global poverty elimination: a belief in the power of audacious questions, and the humility to embrace the answers we find when we ask them.

We used to ask *what is poverty?* We used to ask *what can we do about poverty?* Those are inherently valuable questions; of course they are. Yet, when we instead start by asking *who owns poverty?*, our answers to the other two questions will fundamentally change—forever.

When we ask *who owns poverty?*, our understanding of what poverty is must be shaped by the perspectives and priorities of poor people themselves. That understanding will include many aspects of their poverty, some of which will be subjective. Yet we don't need to worry about whether it's too difficult for us to measure the subjective, or too impolite to ask about sensitive topics, because it's not us doing the measuring. When poor people are allowed to ask themselves difficult questions, unexpected things happen. The first of these is that people take a step up the ladder toward looking at their lives in a new way; a way in which they count their blessings, take stock of their challenges and have a clear vision of what's possible: what it looks like to be non-poor in each aspect of their lives.

To help poor families *continue* to make meaning out of their poverty information, we must avoid the temptation to reduce the richness of multidimensional information into a single index, percentage or poverty score. Poverty indices that aggregate poverty data in this way might be useful for policymakers at the top—but we need to recognize that policymakers aren't the only decision-makers in society, and they can never own someone else's poverty. Family decision-makers, on the other hand, are better served by dashboards that present disaggregated poverty data all in one place at one time. More importantly, the way in which we express what we mean by 'poverty' must be framed from the point of view of the family that owns it: *We are a family that saves. We are a family that has adequate clothing and nutritious food. We are a family that could do a bit better at keeping a family budget.*

When we do this, the question *what can we do about poverty?* answers itself. We know what eliminating poverty looks like: getting to green in everything. We know it's possible because all of the indicators are achievable by the families themselves. We know there are already families in every community beating the odds on every indicator. Information is power. Actionable information is turbo power. A government census empowers the government to act. An extractive research survey empowers an international development NGO to act. I have been all over the world, and I have yet to meet a poor person who can't self-diagnose their own poverty. What they usually lack, however, is the agency and self-efficacy needed to do something about it. If we give them the right tools, every family can be a changemaker.

HOW, THEN, SHOULD WE VIEW our future role in eliminating global poverty? By 'we', I am speaking of all the organizations around the world involved in funding, planning, implementing and advocating for anti-poverty projects—the development industrial complex, for lack of a better all-encompassing term. I refer here to the entire eco-system that surrounds a poverty paradigm that is founded on the wrong questions, and is therefore driven by the wrong answers.

The Poverty Stoplight is as small as one single conversation between a mentor and a family, and as large as a fundamental re-think of how we do development and social change. To date, we have behaved as though we own other people's poverty—and that unexamined assumption has shaped every aspect of what we do, how we do it, and how we describe the notion of success. We set the intellectual agenda, we define the problems, we build the poverty measurement and tracking tools, we design the programs, we raise the money and we report back to our funders on our impact. It doesn't take a leap of imagination, however, to see that when poor people own their own poverty; when they own the responsibility for eliminating that poverty; when theirs is the most important voice in the poverty-elimination process; then our role, our aims, our efforts as development organizations are bound to change.

Please don't misunderstand me. I'm not suggesting for one moment that, by helping families to own their poverty, we're meant to simply hand them their dashboard and get out of the way. I don't believe we should abandon our responsibility toward poor families, nor I am suggesting we place the burden of overcoming poverty entirely on their shoulders. But we will be called upon to work in new ways, to collaborate in new ways and to interact with families in new ways. When poor families start articulating their needs and demanding change, we'd better be ready to respond—in a manner which fully respects their agency, their authority and their self-efficacy.

The most radical vision I can think of for the 'development organization of the future' is one that has zero agenda, zero thematic focus and zero mission—other than to facilitate the change goals defined by families and communities. Imagine what would happen if an organization showed up with nothing but two questions: *What do you need? How can we help you make that happen?* Using the Poverty Stoplight, it could accompany individual families by connecting them to existing solutions and identifying new ones. It could also accompany the community as a whole to demand better from external service providers (by leveraging its size, reputation and connections to get things done). If this is not poverty elimination designed for poor families, and poverty elimination done by poor families, then I don't know what is.

Of course, a world in which social change is done in this way looks completely different from the one we have now—and I'm not necessarily suggesting that we should be heading in that direction. It's interesting to think about, of course, but it's not my role to tell you what the shape of the development industry will be in future. Instead, I would challenge us to keep asking audacious questions, such as 'who owns poverty?', and all the questions that follow on from there.

For instance, we might ask ourselves whether it's actually unhelpful to use the term 'poor neighborhood'. It's a phrase we casually throw about without it being helpful or accurate in any sense. I even recall this phrase being responsible for a heated fight among my staff during the years I served (on leave from the Foundation) as Mayor of Asunción (1996–2001), presiding over a coalition between my own Liberal Party and the Left-leaning *Partido Encuentro Nacional*. The Director of Public Works (a dear friend and collaborator to this day, Raul Gauto) and the Director of Social Services had drawn battle lines over the construction of a bridge. Each claimed responsibility for the project for different reasons; Raul saw the bridge (inasmuch as it was to be made of cement and could be termed 'infrastructure') as a public works project, while the Director of Social Services saw it as a social project by virtue of its location on the map—the city slum (read: poor neighborhood).

Although I didn't articulate it in this way at the time, it was the first moment I recall feeling troubled by a purely geographic definition of poverty. In my work with the Foundation, I had seen thousands of small cottage industries, seamstresses, shopkeepers and poor street vendors all over the city. Never did they remain neatly confined to the slums. Many poor families even lived in what we consider to be 'well-off', middle-class neighborhoods. True, they may have had marginally better homes than the families living in the slums, but that didn't mean they weren't poor and couldn't have benefited from support from the social services department.

The point is: poverty is a lot more unruly than we thought, and it doesn't know how to read maps. Between families in the same community, it doesn't manifest as the same thing in the same way for everyone. We might have suspected this to be true, but we could never have been certain until we had the technology to help families see what was under their noses the whole time—to undertake the equivalent of genetically sequencing household poverty.

By the same logic, we might conclude that there's no such thing as a 'rich neighborhood' either, because lurking in every green forest we'll find a surprising number of reds and yellows. We'll find a man who is earning a decent wage, but his family income is unstable because he's the only one in work and he's on a zero-hour contract—and so they can never plan ahead. Or, we'll find a family in a well-appointed house with wide social networks, but that is experiencing a problem with disordered eating as a means of coping with unhappiness or the pressure to conform to other people's ideals. Or, we'll find a family where both parents are earning an income, but the dynamics of household decision-making are skewed because of a problem with domestic violence. Or all of the above.

When we look at the world in this way, we can dispense with useless distinctions—not only *poor neighborhood* versus *rich neighborhood* and *poor person* versus *rich person*, but also *poor country* versus *rich country*. *Us* versus *them*. We can recognize the fact that – regardless of our country of origin, our color, our creed, our religion, our race, our income level or anything else – every one of us strives to provide for our family, nourish our minds and bodies, participate in our community and dream of a better future. We are all the same; we have an essential oneness.

Does this mean that a poverty-elimination methodology developed in Paraguay is applicable everywhere, from California to Cameroon to China? Yes. Does that mean that poverty in Tallahassee is the same as poverty in Thailand? No. Each of those communities must define what it means to be poor, very poor and not poor in each indicator within their own contexts. What connects them, however, is their shared ability to name their poverty, to own their poverty and to eliminate their poverty using the same methodology—with the support of their mentors, the community and maybe even the whole country.

Here's another audacious question: *what would it take to bring an entire country out of poverty within five years?* I've done the math on my own nation. If we think about Paraguay not as a collection of 7 million inhabitants but as a community of 1.4 million families, and if we retrained 8,000 existing civil servants to become mentors, and if each mentor worked with 180 families each—what would happen?

Of course, not every family would need the same level of input – indeed, not every family would even necessarily need in-person mentoring (we might think about how to harness technology to deploy solutions) – but let's imagine, for a moment, the power of having a multidimensional poverty map of an entire country, and the power of having everyone in the country involved in a national conversation around eliminating poverty. The Ministry of Transport would instantly see where it needed to build new roads and transport links. The Department of Health could deploy nurses to close every single gap in the national program of vaccines in a single month. Banks would have a map showing them where people were locked out of access to financial services. Community groups could see where to run awareness campaigns on healthy cooking or set up new sports leagues.

Imagine if a politician in that country ran for office on a platform of getting everyone to green in 'Water' and

'Roads' during their first term. Imagine if social safety-net programs were redesigned to reimburse families the cost of getting to green in all their housing indicators. Imagine towns that competed to see who could get to green in 'School Attendance' first. Imagine the annual national hackathon where people competed to design the best app for starting government petitions. Or imagine the Ministry of Culture funding a national roadshow of a participatory theatrical event that confronted the issue of domestic violence. What would happen if the government launched a 'national week of respect for differences', during which key messages and pledges were heard from every pulpit, school assembly and company newsletter?

Having taken the Poverty Stoplight to the community level, I really do believe that taking it to the national level would provide both powerful lessons and powerful opportunities to innovate solutions for poverty elimination. And, as it happens, I am not alone in my thinking. As this book went to press, the government of Ecuador launched a pilot to test the Poverty Stoplight as its new national rural poverty-elimination framework. The impetus for this was a chance meeting with Xavier Lazo, who, as I mentioned, is Ecuador's Minister of Agriculture and a former banana exporter. I had been invited to give the keynote speech at EARTH University's graduation ceremony in Costa Rica in December 2018, where he was honored as a distinguished alumnus. Ecuador had historically signed up to the fair trade movement, but Xavier had serious doubts about whether it was making any difference. Learning about the Poverty Stoplight, he asked if he could pay a visit. He, Berenice Cordero (the Minister of Social and Economic Inclusion) and two other colleagues arrived in Cerrito in mid-February 2019. A few weeks later, he sent a team of experts to arrange a technology transfer of the Poverty Stoplight, and the Foundation started work on localizing the indicators and training his team.

Working with the Poverty Stoplight for nearly a decade has also brought me to the point where I articulate questions that others find deeply shocking, such as: *What if there's no such thing as being homeless? What if the problem is actually that people are family-less?* Here's how these questions came about: I was sitting around a table with my friends and colleagues from the Salvation Army in Orange County (California) and the University of California, Irvine (where I am a Visiting Professor). I was listening to the reps from the Salvation Army talk about their fascinating effort to build and provide housing, and the sheer scale of the homelessness problem in the local area.

In response, I mused out loud about the irony of the fact that I come from what they would consider a 'poor country', but that we don't have nearly the same amount of home-lessness as the US, a 'rich country'. Yes, we have inadequate housing stock; yes, we have families squatting on other's peo-ple's land in precarious shelters; and yes, we have poor people who beg for money on a street corner during the day. But you don't see them at night—because they go home. They have homes. So how can it be that we have, on the one hand, a poor country where people don't sleep on the street, and, on the other, a rich country where people do?

To me, the word 'homeless' implies that, simply by giving a homeless person a house, their problems will be solved. But we know that's not true. It's typical to see homeless people living in clusters, in communities, in – dare I say it? – fam-ilies consisting of other homeless people. I'm not talking about their biological families, but it's nonetheless a kind of family—sometimes dysfunctional, but often a place where a person can find support, safety and companionship, where they can share information and resources, because that's what families do for each other.

Now, let's think about what happens when a homeless person is put into a charity shelter and their connection with this street 'family' is severed. How can the shelter create a new supportive family; one that provides the backdrop for a person to get to green not just in housing and health but in everything? Think about it: everything is connected. A glance at the Poverty Stoplight reveals a range of both objective and subjective indicators that could potentially influence whether or not a person has a home and is able to hold down a job, including: 'Good Hygiene', 'Good Nutrition', 'Good Transportation', 'Telephone', 'Clothes', 'Budget', 'Social Support Networks', 'Staying Informed', 'Self-Efficacy' and 'Decision-Making'.

If we recognize the validity of the concept of multidimensional poverty, then we need to stop seeing people's poverty through the lens of a single issue. We, as social-service providers and development organizations, need to start treating people as whole persons. A person is not just homeless. A person is not just income poor. A person is not just politically excluded or illiterate. A person is never *just one thing*.

The example I often share is that of our partner organization in New Orleans called Roots of Renewal. Ostensibly, its programmatic focus is tackling the problems of recidivism and the housing deficit by putting formerly incarcerated young people to work restoring the city's dilapidated housing stock. As part of this, the organization engages in intensive mentoring with its youth, using the Poverty Stoplight.

Kiana Calloway (who runs the mentoring program at Roots of Renewal) explains why: "If you're young and black in this city, you can't find no job. The only way to make a living is to be a criminal. When I was 10, I had a gun. My role models were drug dealers. My role models were armed robbers. My role models were murderers, because that's all my community consisted of at that point. I went to prison at 16 and got out at 34. When I got out, there were no re-entry programs to help me stop seeing myself as a prisoner, and start seeing myself as a citizen. No one to help me find work and no one to help me get my act together. That's why so many of my friends and relatives wound up back in prison after a couple of months. I decided it was on me to change that. I knew that I never wanted to see another Kiana go through what I been through. I'm gonna do everything I can to make sure that, if you're in my grasp, I'm pumping prosperity into you, I'm pumping entrepreneurship into you. I'm pumping the message that you need to do better—not just for you but for your offspring." The day that guys get out of prison is the day that Roots of Renewal starts working with them—and it accompanies them for four months, while they learn construction skills and get certified so they can move on to a good job in the city.

However, as Kiana puts it: "Roots is not just an organization that deals with construction of houses; we deal with construction of the being." The first step is to get the kids to open up about their life before prison—their family, school, community. Then they reflect on what their life was like inside prison—how they felt, what they did. But what he's most interested in is getting them to start talking about what their life is going to be like now; now that they're out of prison for the first time. Kiana uses the Poverty Stoplight to start conversations such as: "What are your stoplights? What is keeping you from getting ahead?" His bottom line is that, if he doesn't help them get past those red lights, it's pretty much a given that the kid will go back to prison. This affects not just them but also the other kids in their family and community, who look to them as role models for how to behave—to see what's possible, and what's worth doing, as a young man of color in New Orleans. As he observes: "We all have things holding us back in life. It could be drugs, it could be not having transportation to get to work. But it's not until we can identify those things, and start talking about them, that we can start dealing with them. We start turning the reds to yellows, and the yellows to green."

I love this story, and I am awed by the work that Roots of Renewal does—not just because it's tackling an urgent social justice issue in the US but also because it refuses to see its kids as anything less than *whole people*.

Now imagine what would happen if every social-purpose organization in the world took a page out of Roots of Renewal's book and started viewing their clients and beneficiaries as whole people. My guess is that they would naturally begin to work with their beneficiaries in an entirely new way, and would define success in an entirely new way.

I'm not suggesting that every single organization becomes a practice expert on every single indicator. Realistically, I wouldn't expect an organization to directly work on more than a handful of issues. But that organization could use the Poverty Stoplight to collaborate with other organizations, using smart partnerships framed around a shared under-standing of multidimensional poverty, powered by shared information in a shared format and working toward a shared goal of helping people become green in everything. Imagine six different NGOs in a city banding together, each taking the lead on one of the six dimensions of the Poverty Stoplight. With technology, it's possible. If we ask audacious questions about poverty, it's possible. And if we keep asking audacious questions about poverty, and have the humility to accept the answers we uncover – even if those answers mean working in radically new ways – then anything is possible.

AS I HOPE WILL BE CLEAR to you by now, the development of the Poverty Stoplight has been, and continues to be, a journey of discovery. Neither Luis Fernando nor I could have ever predicted where we'd end up today, nor can we ever know where we'll be a year from now. This journey began with a simple question – *what is poverty?* – but it didn't end there, and the place we are today isn't thanks to any one single person. So, while I am relating this story through the lens of my own personal experience and perspective, it's important to remember that the Poverty Stoplight represents the accumulated wisdom of hundreds of people around the world—from those sitting in the so-called ivory towers, to those sitting in the so-called slums, and everyone in between.

What the Poverty Stoplight does is to collect those tools, insights, approaches and philosophies and combine them in a new way, based on the much more radical question of *who owns poverty?* We didn't invent anything new—we simply rearranged existing pieces as we found them. We didn't invent the traffic-light method of prioritizing tasks—we simply applied it to poverty indicators. We didn't invent the portable computing device called a tablet—we simply leveraged it to allow poor families to self-diagnose their own multidimensional poverty. We didn't invent the poverty indicators—we simply selected the ones identified as the most meaningful and actionable by poor families themselves. We didn't define the thresholds within each indicator between very poor, poor and non-poor—our clients did. We didn't invent action planning—all we did was to frame it in such a way that the family could lead their own change process.

Technology is changing everything. Technology makes it all possible. Today we are witnessing, in the words of Klaus Schwab, the fourth industrial revolution—one in which artificial intelligence, biotechnology, nanotechnology, robotics and the internet of things are changing the way we work, the way we live, the way we travel, the way we collaborate, the way we participate, and the way we claim our agency and voice within a world that increasingly puts the individual center stage.

Not only that, but the economy of the future will rise and fall based on not who controls the capital but who has the human talent required to create and innovate in an increasingly complex world. Global poverty is a problem to be solved, and we need the best brains to show up to that challenge.

Yet, if we're excluding poor people from the production of poverty knowledge and solutions, we're missing out on a lot of potential talent. Can we really afford not to listen to the experts?

In recognition of this, let me affirm that individuals are the real heroes of this book, and of the Poverty Stoplight. Not me, not the Foundation, not our partners and not the development organizations stepping into this new landscape of poverty thinking and practice.

The real heroes are the family decision-makers who are empowered to take control of their lives—who have the opportunity and the obligation to do so. They now have a magnifying glass they can use to examine their lives to see what was right under their noses this whole time, to name the things that are holding them back and to give them a clear vision of what is possible to do—and worth doing.

That's not to say that the path toward improved well-being will always be straightforward. There will be moments in our lives when our green lights turn yellow or red, and not always for tangible reasons. Sometimes, it's that we're more willing to be honest with ourselves about the things that could be better in our lives. I know that's true in my own life, and I'm willing to bet it's true in yours. Our situation and our awareness of our situation are two different things, orbiting each other in ways we can't always predict. But this I can say: Once we know, we can't *un*know. Once we see what's possible, what being non-poor in an indicator looks like, we can't *un*see it.

At the end of the day, that's all that the Poverty Stoplight really is: information and the dignity of choice. Isn't that all anyone could wish for in life? To not be held captive to someone else's definition of who we are? To understand that the power to improve our lives is in our hands, and have a custom-made map to guide us? To not feel like we have to wait for someone else to swoop down and sort out our problems? In some cases, this might lead a family to demand-ing better of itself; in others, it might mean demanding better of external service providers.

If we accept that the principle underlying the Poverty Stoplight is the means to meaningfully choose, then we must accept it's about choosing not only *what* to prioritize but also *whether* to prioritize. For instance, we might meet a grand-mother who decides that, while having a complete picture of her strengths and weaknesses, her priority will not be to get from yellow to green in 'Income', because she wants to spend more time with her grandchildren instead. For her, the Poverty Stoplight can be about the freedom, as Amartya Sen suggests, to make informed choices in line with her values. I might decide that, in this particular time in my life, investing in my children's education is more important than my own savings account balance. As I said: the power of information; the dignity of choice.

So, too, are the lines of sight changing. In traditional, top-down development approaches, families were forced to look up. They looked up to the government to solve their prob-lems. They looked up to the charity or NGO that distributed goods and services. Decisions about what to do, where, when and why were made upstream, rather than by the families themselves.

The Poverty Stoplight empowers families to look not just within but across to other families in the same community to source solutions. Across to other families that are beating the odds; across to families with access to relevant resources and insights, motivation and inspiration. Families will be able to not only accompany each other to tackle their deprivations but also connect the dots and leverage their information and voices to make things happen at a broader level. This is vital because, while the Stoplight frames poverty from the point of view of the family and defines behaviors the family can do to tackle their deprivations, structural drivers of poverty still exist, and those economic, social and political factors impact on how much progress we can make as families and communities who eliminate our own poverty.

Deindustrialization, tax avoidance, inflation, unemployment, underemployment, low wages, low-quality education, racism, sexism, ableism—without a doubt, these frame and influence our experience of well-being at a family level. Of course they do. That's why the Poverty Stoplight contains an 'Organization and Participation' dimension encompassing whether a family is informed, respects human rights and differences, joins groups, lobbies the government, votes and engages in problem-solving.

Civil society needs to hold the government to account, and that pressure for accountability will be at its strongest when driven by real-time granular information about an issue. Imagine empowering families to connect with other families across the country that are all suffering from the same injustice, or dealing with the same deprivation. What would happen if they could speak as one? Injustices persist when they are invisible. Structural issues run deep; they take time and effort to fix. Now imagine what we could accomplish if everyone in the country showed up to protest or support an issue and was empowered to work together to demand change from those in office. Empowered individuals make for empowered communities, and citizen activism is a powerful tool for driving the kinds of policy-level and societal change needed to make it possible for families to eliminate their poverty.

I am poverty; you are poverty. We are all poverty and not-poverty in our own unique ways. I am Martín Burt, and my family has three reds and five yellows. While it's vital that we see each other as unique, multidimensional, complicated and often contradictory human beings, let's also recognize our *wholeness*, our *oneness*. Technology makes it possible, but we still need to muster the moral imagination to make it happen.

We are all on the same journey to do better, to get green and then keep going because we know we can, and because we know it's worth it. The world is changing. The weight of responsibility for eliminating global poverty is shifting. How will you respond?

ANNEXES

LIST OF ACRONYMS

ADEC	Paraguayan Association of Christian Entrepreneurs
CSR	Corporate Social Responsibility
GNP	Gross national product
HDI	Human Development Index
HP	Hewlett-Packard
HR	Human resources
MDG(s)	Millennium Development Goal(s)
MPI	Multidimensional Poverty Index
NGO	Non-governmental organization
OPHI	Oxford Poverty and Human Development Initiative
PPP	Purchasing power parity
PWR	Participatory Wealth Ranking
SDG(s)	Sustainable Development Goal(s)
UN	United Nations
UNDP	United Nations Development Program
UNICEF	United Nations Children's Fund (originally United Nations International Children's Emergency Fund)
USAID	United States Agency for International Development

POVERTY STOPLIGHT
(PARAGUAY VERSION)
DIMENSIONS & INDICATORS

Income & Employment
1. We have enough income
2. We have savings
3. We have access to credit
4. We have different sources of income
5. We have forms of ID

Health & Environment
6. We live in an unpolluted environment
7. We manage our garbage well
8. We have running water
9. We have access to health services
10. We have a nutritious diet
11. We have good hygiene
12. We have good sexual health
13. We have a healthy smile
14. We have good eye health
15. We are vaccinated
16. We have insurance

Housing & Infrastructure
17. We have a safe home
18. We have a comfortable home
19. We have separate bedrooms

20. We have an equipped kitchen
21. We have an adequate bathroom
22. We have a refrigerator and other appliances
23. We have a phone
24. We have clothes to change everyday
25. We are safe from violence
26. We have not been robbed
27. We have electricity
28. We have regular transportation
29. We have accessible roads

Education & Culture
30. Our children go to school
31. We know how to read and write
32. We have school supplies
33. We have a budget
34. We know how to generate income
35. We have access to information
36. We have hobbies
37. We respect differences
38. We respect human rights
39. Our children don't work

Organization & Participation
40. We are part of a group
41. We know how to contact public officials
42. We solve our own problems
43. We vote in elections

Mind & Motivation
44. We have a family life plan
45. I feel confident
46. We make decisions together
47. We control our emotions
48. We have no violence in our family
49. We have an entrepreneurial spirit
50. I have control over my life decisions

ABOUT THE AUTHOR

Dr. Martín Burt is Founder and Chief Executive Officer of *Fundación Paraguaya*, a non-profit devoted to the promotion of social entrepreneurship and economic self-reliance to eliminate poverty around the world. He is a pioneer in applying new poverty metrics, microfinance, micro-franchise, youth entrepreneurship, financial literacy and financially self-sufficient agricultural technical vocational methodologies. Dr. Burt is currently a board member of the Schwab Foundation for Social Entrepreneurship at the World Economic Forum, the Global Foodbanking Network, and Teach A Man To Fish. He is Co-Founder of the Bertoni Environmental Foundation, Asociación Paraguaya de la Calidad, Paraguay Educa, Club Universitario de Rugby de Asunción, Sistema B Paraguay, and the Mbaracayú Forest Foundation. In public service, he has served as Chief of Staff to the President of Paraguay, was elected Mayor of Asunción, and appointed Vice Minister of Commerce. Dr. Burt has written books on economics, development, municipal government, poetry and education. He has received awards from organizations including Avina Foundation, Skoll Foundation, Schwab Foundation, Synergos, the Eisenhower Fellowship, the Inter-American Development Bank, the World Innovation Summit for Education, and Nestlé. He is a graduate of the University of the Pacific and George Washington University. He holds a PhD from Tulane University, and is a Visiting Professor of Social Entrepreneurship at Worcester Polytechnic Institute, and Distinguished Visiting Professor at University of California, Irvine. Dr. Burt was born in Asunción, Paraguay in 1957 where he resides with his family.

ACKNOWLEDGMENTS

I want to fully acknowledge and recognize the support and guidance that I have received from many people while developing the Poverty Stoplight and writing this book.

First and foremost, I want to thank the more than 80,000 families and our partners from more than 250 organizations who have self-diagnosed using the Poverty Stoplight and who have developed their 'life maps' to overcome their challenges. These families are not only from Paraguay, but also from our hubs in Argentina, Chile, Colombia, Honduras, Indonesia, Mexico, Nigeria, Papua New Guinea, Philippines, Sierra Leone, Singapore, South Africa, United Kingdom and the United States, as well as from our special projects in Bolivia, Brazil, Burundi, China, Costa Rica, Dominican Republic, Ecuador, Guatemala, India, Indonesia, El Salvador, Kenya, Nicaragua, Pakistan, Peru, Philippines, Puerto Rico, Senegal, Taiwan, Tanzania, and Uganda.

Second, I want to thank members and directors of *Fundación Paraguaya* for their friendship and unwavering support: Amado Adorno, Julio Alvarado, Jose Antonio Bergues, Guido Britez, Luis Breuer, Esteban Burt, Paula Burt, Alvaro Caballero, Sara Centurión, Gabriel Cosp, Diana Diaz de Espada, Daniel Elicetche, Antonio Espinoza, Ruben Fadlala, Maria Gracia Gauto, Raul Gauto, Marcos Goldenberg, Astrid Gustafson, Eduardo Gustale, Pablo Herken, Peter Jones, Cathy Kelly, Margarita Kelly, Enrique Landó, Marta Lane, Eduardo Manchini, Fernando Peroni, Francisca Peroni, Guillermo Peroni, Pascual Rubiani, Yan Speranza, Jorge Talavera, Ramiro Rodriguez Alcalá, and Roberto Urbieta.

Third, I want to thank staff at *Fundación Paraguaya*, particularly my long-time colleague and friend Luis Fernando Sanabria, our General Manager, as well as Celsa Acosta, Lourdes Aguero, Narumi Akita, Juan Carlos Aldama, Ismael Alonso, Telma Alvarenga, Adriana Alvarez, Elena Alvarez, Luis Antonelli, Lorenzo Arrúa, Rodrigo Alonso, Limpia Baez, Lorena Benítez, Safira Benítez, Sandra Cano, Fabiola Cantero, Andrés Carrizosa, Alejandro Carrizosa, Adalia Castillo, Luis Cateura, Marcos Cespedes, Minociene Cherestal, Julia Corvalán, Lilian Duarte, Mónica Eisenkolbl, Emilio Espínola, Gabriel Fadlala, Patricia Fernández, Jaime Ferreira, Carlos Filártiga, Hugo Florentin, Rosa García, Roberto Gimenez, Juan Fernando Gómez, Cesar González, Dionisio González, Katharina Hammler, Sara Hooper, Ignacio Jiménez, Laina John, Kelly Jones, Mary Liz Kehler, Fanny Larue, Cecilia López, Juan Manuel Machado, Stephanie Manciagli, Tania Martínez, Silvia Meza, Neyda Millan, Cecilia Monges, Arnaldo Moreira, Sediwilka Morilla, Patricia Oliver, Claudia Ortega, Silvana Ortega, Stacy Pendeville, Elena Pérez, Fernando Pfannl, Zaida Ramirez, Nancy Ramos, Cosima Reichenbach, Luis Resquin, Miguel Angel Rivarola, Ana Paula Rojas, Guido Ruiz Diaz, Ada Sachelaridi, Jose Luis Salomón, Omar Sanabria, Walter Sánchez, Bjorn Schmidke, Milva Schup, Verse Shom, Cristian Sosa, Veronica Teme, Nora Torales, Bruno Vaccotti, Karen Valdez, Jimena Vallejos, Lucas Vera, Pedro Villalba and Eri Yegros.

Fourth, I want to thank my editor and publisher Katherine Knotts who helped me write this book. Without her I simply couldn't have done it.

Fifth, I want to thank my wife Dorothy as well as Georgie, Vanessa, George, Tommy, Marie-Claire, Juanqui, Eleonor, Naomi, Paul, Siena and Brielle whose love, patience, support, and inspiration keep me going, always enthusiastic and optimistic about the future.

Last but not least, I want to thank friends, social entrepreneurs, mentors and donors without whose leadership, inspiration, constructive criticism, and support my team and I would have never traveled the Poverty Stoplight discovery journey. While no such list can ever be complete, I would like to extend particular thanks to: Sabina Alkire, Diran Apelian, Roberto Artavia, Rick Aubry, José Ignacio Avalos, Rodrigo Baggio, Indranil Banerjee, John Bell,

William Bertrand, Jeroo Billimoria, Brizio Biondi, Taddy Blecher, François Bonnici, Ana Botero, Aquilino Bravo, Bill Burrus, Carl Byker, Vivian Cajé, Mercedes Camperi, Elena Casolari, Carlos Castello, Arachu Castro, Alex Cobo, Vicky Colbert, Arturo Condo, Vera Cordeiro, Carmen Cosp, Colin Crawford, Enda Curran, George De Lama, David Dewez, Peggy Dulany, Christopher Dunford, Paul Ellingstad, Margee Ensign, Ludovico Feoli, Xoan Fernández, Matt Flannery, Willy Foote, Federico Franco, Luis Fretes, Paul Fritz, Jim Fruchterman, Alan Gilbertson, Michael Green, Jürgen Griesbeck, Simon Graffy, Joseph Grenny, Steve Gross, Nancy Guerra, Isabel Guerrero, Diego Guzmán, Victoria Hale, John Hammock, Pamela Hartigan, Arthur Heinricher, Steven Hendrix, Sandy Herz, Jerry Hildebrand, Gail Hochachka, Charles Jillings, Hans Jöhr, Nik Kafka, Jordan Kassalow, James Koch, Enrique Lavernia, Joe Madiath, Barbara Magnoni, Todd Manwaring, Richard Matthew, Bill Maurer, Katherine Milligan, Lisa Moon, Nicola Morganti, Gonzalo Muñoz, Laura Murphy, Soledad Nuñez, Susana Ortiz, Maria Otero, Sally Osberg, Dave Peery, Edmund Phelps, Maria Adelaida Quevedo, Larry Reed, Paul Rice, Bunker Roy, Albina Ruiz, Amitabha Sadangi, Soraya Salti, Stanley Samarasinghe, Duncan Saville, Ubaldo Scavone, Premal Shah, Michael Schlein, Stephan Schmidheiney, Mirjam Schoening, J.B. Schramm, Caroline Schuster, Hilde Schwab, Klaus Schwab, Gary Shearer, Jeff Sheets, Jack Sim, Jeff Skoll, Dauphine Sloan, Nina Smith, Guillermo Sosa, Dorothy Stoneman, Luis Szarán, Pierre Tami, Karen Tse, Robert Traver, Carmen Velasco, Michael Walton, Bart Weetjens, Gary White, Ken Wilber, Kris Wobbe, Sakena Yacoobi, and Kyle Zimmer.

FURTHER INFORMATION

About the Poverty Stoplight

Visit **povertystoplight.org** to learn more about the Poverty Stoplight metric and methodology—what it is, how it works, where it's being used and what's happening as a result. You can learn more about our team, our partners and supporters. You can also see samples of the Life Map and watch videos that show the Poverty Stoplight in action around the world.

About the Foundation

Head to **fundacionparaguaya.org.py** for an overview of the work of the Foundation. There, you'll find information about our microfinance, agricultural schools and entrepreneurship education programs. You can also meet our team and see where we're working around the world, and the amazing changemakers we collaborate with to achieve our mission.

HOW TO MAKE CHIPAS
(GLUTEN-FREE)

Ingredients

1 ¼ cups (125g) grated salty hard cheese (e.g. parmesan or grana padano)
1 ¼ cups (125g) grated soft cheese, not salty (e.g. gouda or fontina)
2 cups (250 g) tapioca starch
¼ tsp table salt
3.5 fl. oz (100 ml) milk
1 egg, beaten

Method

Preheat the oven to 375°F (190 °C). In a large bowl, lightly toss dry ingredients until cheese is coated. Add wet ingredients and knead to form a smooth dough which is not sticky to the touch. Add more starch if needed to create a smooth consistency, without overworking your dough. Avoid letting your dough become too warm, or it won't rise properly in the oven.

Turn the dough onto a clean surface and divide into four portions. Roll each portion into a six-inch log and cut into six even 1-inch pieces. Place coins on a sheet lined with baking parchment and bake for 15-20 minutes until the bottom is browned and the top has taken on a hard, golden sheen with dark spots.

Serve warm, and enjoy.

INDEX

red